PROTECTING DONOR INTENT

PROTECTING DONOR INTENT

HOW TO DEFINE AND SAFEGUARD YOUR PHILANTHROPIC PRINCIPLES

JEFFREY J. CAIN

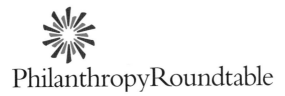

PhilanthropyRoundtable

Published by The Philanthropy Roundtable, 1730 M Street NW, Suite 601, Washington, DC, 20036.

Free copies of this book are available to qualified donors. To learn more, or to order more copies, call (202) 822-8333, email main@philanthropyroundtable.org, or visit philanthropyroundtable.org. An e-book version is available from major online booksellers. A PDF may be downloaded at no charge at philanthropyroundtable.org.

ISBN 978-0-9851265-0-6
LCCN 2012932753

First printing, February 2012

TABLE OF CONTENTS

FOREWORD
Why Donors Must Protect
Their Philanthropic Principles

The Philanthropy Roundtable is delighted to publish this guidebook by Jeffrey Cain on how donors can define and safeguard their philanthropic principles. With this guidebook, we hope to help philanthropists to think through the best strategies for carrying out their charitable purposes and core values.

The need for such a guidebook is clear. All too often the trustees and staff of grantmaking institutions pay little attention to the principles governing their founders' charitable giving. Indeed, one can imagine that in many cases the initial donors would never have created their foundations if they knew then what would later be funded in their names.

For example, oil magnate J. Howard Pew established the J. Howard Pew Freedom Trust (one of seven trusts making up the Pew Charitable Trusts) in 1957 to "acquaint the American people" with "the evils of bureaucracy," "the values of a free market," and "the paralyzing effects of government controls on the lives and activities of people," and to "inform our people of the struggle, persecution, hardship, sacrifice and death by which freedom of the individual was won." Admirers and critics alike of Pew's recent signature initiatives—such as its crusades for campaign finance regulation, universal early childhood education, and recognition of the dangers of global climate change—can agree that in the past two decades, with the exception of its emphasis on religion in public life, J. Howard's worldview and philanthropic goals have played little role in informing Pew's strategy and charitable giving.

Of course, founding donors themselves are often partly to blame for departures from their principles. Instructions have frequently been so open-ended that future trustees have very little guidance in setting philanthropic strategy. John D. MacArthur gave his trustees no instructions at all. "I'll make [the money]," he told them. "You people, after I'm dead, will have to learn how to spend it." John D. Rockefeller's mission for the Rockefeller Foundation was "to improve the well-being of mankind throughout the world," a charge that could justify just about any philanthropic expenditure. Andrew Carnegie left one instruction to the Carnegie Corporation: to provide pensions to American presidents and their widows. Otherwise, he wrote: "I give my Trustees full authority to change policy or causes hitherto aided . . . They shall best conform to my wishes by using their own judgment."*

The Ford Foundation is the best known example of donor neglect. Henry Ford had a fairly well-articulated philosophy of giving, both in his writings and interviews—e.g., "I do not believe in giving folks things. I do believe in giving them a chance to make things for themselves"—and in the record of his generous contributions during his lifetime to organizations such as Henry Ford Hospital, historic Greenfield Village, and the Anti-Cigarette League of the United States and Canada. However, in his documents establishing the Ford Foundation, he left no instructions on its philanthropic purposes. Indeed, there is compelling evidence that Henry Ford created his foundation principally to maintain family control of the Ford Motor Company. How it was supposed to give out its money he did not say.

Henry's grandson, Henry Ford II, was later to write his famous 1977 resignation letter from the Ford Foundation board. "The foundation is a creature of capitalism," he wrote, "a statement that, I'm sure, would be shocking to many professional staff people in the field of philanthropy. It is hard to discern recognition of this fact in anything the foundation does. It is even more difficult to find an understanding of this in many of the institutions, particularly the universities, that are the beneficiaries of the foundation's grant programs . . . I'm not playing the role of the hard-headed tycoon who thinks all philanthropoids are Socialists and all university professors are Communists. I'm just suggesting to the trustees and the staff that the system that makes the foundation possible very probably is worth preserving."

The irony is that the Ford family could have shaped the philosophical and philanthropic direction of the Ford Foundation but voluntarily abdicated this role. Henry Ford II was chairman of the Ford Foundation during its first decade as the foundation began its ideological transformation to the left, and he and his brother initially controlled a majority of the Ford Foundation board. His priority, however, was his 34-year chairmanship of the Ford Motor Company; his attention to the foundation was more limited and sporadic.

If Henry Ford II allowed the philosophical transformation of the Ford Foundation through relative neglect, at some other foundations family members actively led the way. The initial board of the MacArthur Foundation was described by one of its members as "mostly a bunch of Midwestern businessmen devoted to free enterprise and opposed to more government controls." However, the founder's son, Rod, much more liberal than his father, was able to seize control of the board and shape much of the foundation's future direction. Members of the Pew family on the board of the Pew Charitable Trusts have generally been supportive of the trusts' new strategies.

Departures from donor intent are not simply ideological. In 2012, the Barnes Foundation will be moving its extraordinary collection of impressionist and post-impressionist masterpieces to a new Philadelphia museum substantially different in character from the intimate art school envisioned by Dr. Albert Barnes. In 2008, Princeton University agreed to pay $100 million to settle a lawsuit charging that the university was ignoring the mission of the Robertson Foundation that established and substantially funded the Woodrow Wilson graduate school: preparing students for government service, especially in international affairs.

In order to help donors understand and avoid such problems, The Philanthropy Roundtable suggests the following guidelines for donors who want to safeguard their philanthropic principles:

- Clearly define your charitable mission. Write it down in your founding documents. Supplement your mission statement with a long written or oral record about your likes and dislikes in charitable giving.

- Choose trustees and staff who share your fundamental principles. Choose family members, friends, and close business associates such as lawyers, bankers, and accountants only if they fit into this category.

- If possible, separate your philanthropic interests from your interests in maintaining control of your company. Donor intent frequently suffers when the two are mixed.

- Give generously while living, and strongly consider a sunset provision for your foundation, perhaps a generation or two after your death.

- If you do establish a foundation in perpetuity, establish procedures for electing future trustees who share your principles, and for encouraging future boards to consider respect for donor intent as part of their fiduciary duty.

—Adam Meyerson
President
The Philanthropy Roundtable

---

* An excellent survey of the abuses of donor intent, many of them self-inflicted, can be found in Martin Morse Wooster's *The Great Philanthropists and the Problem of "Donor Intent"* (Capital Research Center: 3rd edition, 2007).

CHAPTER 1
An Introduction to Donor Intent

This guidebook is intended to offer practical advice to philanthropists who want to ensure that the assets they dedicate to charity are disbursed as they intend. It identifies common pitfalls, explains the relevant tradeoffs, and offers detailed descriptions of successful strategies for safeguarding donor intent. It lays a broad range of options before you, and suggests ways of defining, securing, and perpetuating your charitable intentions.

What this guidebook is *not* intended to do is provide specific information for executing governing instruments, applying for tax-exempt status, or completing state filings. Those are issues best left to expert legal counsel, who can address your specific needs. Similarly, this guidebook is neither an elaborate theoretical justification for donor intent nor an exhaustive history of the many instances in which charitable institutions have violated the clear wishes of their benefactors. While those are all worthy topics, the purpose of this guidebook is more down-to-earth. It intends to serve as a practical resource for successful individuals who want to think clearly about the future of the assets they plan to dedicate to charity.

Why Donor Intent Matters

If you intend to dedicate large sums of money to charity, you should think hard about what purpose you want that money to serve. If you intend to have others collaborate in your philanthropic giving, especially after your death, you should not assume that your successors will instinctively understand your wishes. Moreover, even if they understand your wishes, you should not assume that they will necessarily want to be constrained by them. If your intentions as a donor are to be respected, you need to clarify what you want your assets to accomplish and create safeguards that help ensure their intended disposition.

You ignore donor intent at your peril. Insufficient planning for future philanthropic efforts can lead to catastrophic consequences. Philanthropists have left fortunes to charitable purposes, only to have their money go to causes they would have opposed. In some cases, their assets were put to uses that would have made them sick. The history of modern philanthropy involves a sad litany of one great foundation after another ignoring—and in some cases violating—the most cherished principles of their founders. Poor planning has likewise contributed to the destruction of families, as various relatives fight over what they believe to be the intended purpose of the funds. At its worst, insufficient attention to donor intent has made the legacy of intelligent and generous individuals into cautionary case studies. On occasion, it has turned a well-meaning, intelligent, and generous philanthropist into a punchline.

But deviations from donor intent are not necessarily quite so dramatic. Donor intent can be compromised by a simple lack of clarity about the purpose of the donated assets—a vacuum that is inevitably filled by the interests and enthusiasms of succeeding boards and staff. In fact, most deviations from the original donor's intentions are not the result of conspiracy or malice. They are more often than not a consequence of largely preventable issues like ill-conceived plans for leadership succession or unclear, inadequate, or contradictory instructions. To keep your resources dedicated to the causes you care about the most, it is essential that you take pains to define your mission and safeguard the means of its execution.

There are other, perhaps slightly more abstract, reasons to think carefully about defining and securing your intent. Every violation of donor intent creates a marginal disincentive for future philanthropy. Deviations from donor intent do not occur in a vacuum. Rather, they inevitably affect the decisions and behavior of other philanthropists. If a donor's friends and colleagues see his money going to causes and groups that they believe he would disapprove of, will they be more or less likely to dedicate funds to charity? At some level, a lack of foresight and planning may serve to decrease the overall amount of charitable giving by individuals and families.

At a still deeper level, violations of donor intent call into question the very assumptions that make possible American civil society. When donor intent is violated, and particularly when it is egregiously violated, it undermines the bedrock trust on which all charitable giving rests. At the heart of the American tradition of generous giving is a respect for the dignity of each individual. That respect in turn makes possible many of the voluntary associations that enrich and strengthen our democratic culture. Violations of donor intent thus weaken our nation's proud tradition of voluntary private initiative and erode American civil society.

Donor Intent vs. Grant Compliance

Before proceeding, it is important to clarify what we mean by donor intent. Donor intent, as we use the term, is primarily concerned with ensuring that a grantmaking organization understands and acts on the vision of its founding benefactor. Those entrusted with the responsibility of disbursing charitable resources have a moral obligation to distribute the assets in the manner they believe most consistent with the intent of the original donor.

Donor intent is related to, but distinct from, grant compliance. Grant compliance is a matter of ensuring fidelity to the terms of a specific charitable gift. A donor—individual or institutional—may make a grant to a nonprofit on the expectation that the recipient will use the grant for specific, defined purposes.

It is the moral responsibility of the nonprofit grant recipient to deploy those assets in a good-faith manner most consistent with the terms of the grant.

The distinction between donor intent and grant compliance is not always obvious. (Supporting organizations and operating foundations—both addressed in Chapter 4—involve, in some sense, issues regarding both donor intent and grant compliance, as the terms are defined here.) That is because both donor intent and grant compliance involve a relationship of trust—the former, between the original donor and those entrusted with signature authority over his checkbook; the latter, between a grantmaker and a grant recipient. Indeed, in everyday conversation, the terms "donor intent" and "grant compliance" are sometimes used interchangeably.

This guidebook is concerned first and foremost with donor intent. It is principally intended for donors who are thinking about establishing a charitable giving entity and who want to preserve their intent, as well as for trustees, directors, or family members looking to recover donor intent in the charitable entity for which they are responsible.

Thinking Ahead

For many philanthropists, donor intent is an afterthought. Many grantmaking entities are established with vague missions, muddled succession plans, and few, if any, accountability mechanisms. Unfortunately, too few philanthropists take the trouble to incorporate into their founding documents the details and language necessary to assist future generations in making operational their charitable intent.

All of this is quite understandable. Many donors put off being specific about their intent because they want to avoid unpleasant conversations—conversations about mortality, about letting go of hard-won assets, about making decisions that might upset members of (often extended or complicated) families. But the fact that these conversations are unpleasant does not mean that they are unnecessary.

By taking time to carefully consider a range of strategies for securing your philanthropic intentions, you are an exception. By understanding your options today for securing donor intent in the future, you are not only taking the necessary first step for advancing your philanthropic legacy. You are also helping your family, associates, and future directors to understand and carry out the mission you set for them.

Guidelines for Ensuring Grant Compliance

Grant compliance is an important concern for all donors. This is not the place for an exhaustive treatment of grant compliance, but it is appropriate to list a few principles that should guide thinking about how to oversee and manage grants made to public charities.

First, become familiar with the organization to which you are making a grant. Get to know its mission, leadership, and programs. Make site visits. Depending on your level of commitment to the organization, get involved in the life of the organization by attending its activities, programs, and functions. Do you feel comfortable entrusting this organization with your charitable gift? Compare this organization to like organizations working in the same or similar field. Do your homework and get involved.

Second, recognize that over time institutions and the people who run them change. As such, consider making a grant for a specific period of time rather than an open-ended grant or endowment gift. For numerous reasons, organizations over time cannot always live up to the terms of a gift. Some organizations simply go out of business. Making a long-term commitment to an organization while restricting your gift to annual grants based on performance gives you maximum leverage in terms of grant compliance.

Third, depending on the nature of your gift, ensure that there is a gift contract or grant agreement in place. There are many examples of gift contracts, some more complicated than others. Grant agreements can help to ensure that both parties have a clear understanding of expectations and they can also outline in advance a means of resolving disagreements.

Fourth, you may consider making your gift through an intermediary organization that will serve to enforce your intentions over time. A third-party organization can ensure compliance standards in your absence prior to disbursing funds. Likewise, you may also consider establishing successor beneficiary organizations that act as backup grantees if the original grant recipient fails to live up to the terms of the original gift agreement.

Finally, it is important to understand the limitations associated with making a grant. Even with a gift agreement, once you make the grant, the money is no longer yours. It is much easier and more effective to establish a good working relationship with an organization prior to making a gift, than it is to try, after the fact, to enforce compliance when outcomes may not be as rosy as you expected or as you were promised. It can take time, even years, to understand what you can realistically achieve through your grantmaking within a given field or with a particular organization or group of organizations. Many donors make large gifts early on that they later come to regret. Take time to learn about the field in which you are working, the people and institutions doing the work, and try to formulate realistic expectations grounded in experience rather than slick marketing brochures, attractive websites, or utopian ideas about what your gift can accomplish.

CHAPTER 2
Choosing a Timeframe
for Donating Assets to Charity

There are three principal timeframes in which you can donate assets to charity:

1. Make charitable contributions while you are alive;
2. Arrange for the disbursement of your assets after your death but before a specific date or event; or
3. Create or endow an entity that is intended to exist in perpetuity.

These three options are not mutually exclusive. You can make extensive charitable contributions within your lifetime *and* create a sunsetting entity *and* establish a perpetual entity. Nevertheless, these are the three basic timeframes in which charitable giving can be conducted. From the perspective of donor intent, there are advantages and disadvantages to each. Donors should think carefully about what they hope to achieve before adopting any one of these strategies.

Giving While Living

If you disburse all of the assets you intend to give to charity within your lifetime, you will have effectively taken care of the issue of donor intent. After all, if there are no assets to entrust to others to disburse, there is no issue of donor intent.

You will, of course, have to grapple with the similar issue of *grant compliance*—ensuring that the charities you fund use your assets for their intended purposes. As every donor knows, grantees may or may not use contributions for their intended purposes. Or as donors learn more about their grantees, they may decide they want to work with other organizations or in different funding areas. Grant compliance is related to donor intent, but it is not quite the same as establishing the parameters within which your successors are to distribute your assets. (For more on grant compliance, please see pages 4–5.)

Giving while living resolves the issue of donor intent, narrowly understood. Again, this is not to suggest that grantees will always perform to your expectations if you spend down during your lifetime; it is possible to feel enormously frustrated with your grant recipients in the process of spending down. It is rather to say that if you disburse all of your charitable assets within your lifetime, you will not have to create mechanisms to govern the distribution of your assets after your death.

There is another important reason why many donors decide to complete their philanthropic giving during their lifetimes. They often sense that their money will go much further if it is spent immediately, on pressing problems. These philanthropists want to be personally involved in the programs they support, investing their time and business acumen—in addition to their wealth—to address the problems of today. They tend to be confident that later generations will make and disburse new fortunes to address future challenges.

Furthermore, if you spend down your charitable resources during your lifetime, you do not have to confront the potential problems associated with creating a grant-making entity that will survive you. For example, there is a tendency among grant-making organizations to drift away from a founding donor's vision and toward conformity with industry trends and staff preferences. That drift need not be inevitable—indeed, one purpose of this guidebook is to provide strategies for its prevention—but it is nevertheless unmistakable. To the extent that donors spend down their charitable resources within their lifetimes, the issue is taken off the table.

Giving while living likewise avoids another problem common among grant-makers whose founding donors are no longer in a position to control them: the emphasis on asset growth rather than grantmaking. Institutional grantmakers have institutional imperatives, foremost among which is the preservation of the institution. While this tendency can be mitigated by date-certain sunset provisions, it remains pronounced among entities that have perpetuity as a founda-

Charles Feeney and the Atlantic Philanthropies

Charles ("Chuck") Feeney is perhaps the leading example of a donor who is committed to spending down his fortune within his own lifetime. Feeney co-founded the Duty Free Shoppers Group, and gave away some $5.5 billion between 1982 and 2011. As of 2011, he planned to spend the remaining $2 billion of the Atlantic Philanthropies' assets by the end of 2016, and close its doors by 2020. When it shuts down, the Atlantic Philanthropies will be the largest foundation in history to spend itself out of existence. "Today's needs are so great and varied," says Feeney, "that intelligent philanthropic support and positive interventions can have greater value and impact today than if they are delayed when the needs are greater." Or, as he sometimes puts it, "If I have $10 in my pocket, and I do something with it today, it's already producing $10 worth of good."

tional goal. If your board has a fiduciary duty to perpetuate your philanthropy into the indeterminate future, it is unsurprising and perhaps inevitable that its focus will gravitate away from grantmaking and toward asset preservation.

(Indeed, a related institutional problem can afflict the grantmaking activities of many institutional donors: bureaucratic sclerosis. The pathologies to which largely unaccountable organizations are susceptible have been known to plague grantmaking organizations. Again, donors who spend down during their lifetimes are often less susceptible to the problem. "I think the worst thing that can happen is to wind up creating a foundation with 500 people in a skyscraper writing each other reports," explains Patrick Byrne, chairman and CEO of Overstock.com. "I certainly didn't work this hard to create something like that.")

And, of course, even within an organization that stays committed to its founding donor's vision, cultural and social changes can render the mission obsolete, no matter how forward-looking or principled its original purpose. Diseases can be cured, social ills can decline and even disappear. When Robert Richard Randall died in June 1801, for example, the New York sea captain and merchant left a considerable sum of money for the purpose of creating a "haven for aged, decrepit, and worn-out sailors." Randall's bequest, intended to be perpetual, gave rise to Sailor's Snug Harbor on Staten Island, which by the late-19th century housed more than 1,000 retired sailors on an 83-acre campus with a working farm, dairy, bakery, chapel, hospital, conservatory, and cemetery. By the 1950s, with only about 200 residents remaining, the facility had fallen into such disrepair that it was taken over by the New York City Landmarks Commission. (The retired sailors were moved to North Carolina.) Snug Harbor has since reopened as a cultural center and botanical garden—worthy causes, to be sure, but completely unrelated to the vision of Captain Randall.

Sunsetting

It is not always practical or desirable to disburse all of your charitable dollars within your lifetime. Your giving may be focused on problems that you think will become more critical in the near future. You may be committed to helping a start-up organization build its capacity for some number of years, extending perhaps beyond your lifetime. Or, more fundamentally, it simply may not be feasible to spend all your philanthropic assets while you are alive. In these cases, it may make sense to create a limited-lifespan grantmaking entity that will survive you for a predetermined length of time.

From the perspective of donor intent, a limited-life grantmaking entity can have certain advantages over perpetual entities. Perhaps chief among them is that the founding donor frequently gets to choose the board that will lead the foundation over the course of its existence. (Indeed, for that reason many donors who create limited-life entities deliberately choose board members a generation younger than themselves.) In many, perhaps most, cases, the board will be populated by people who personally knew the founder, who knew his likes and dislikes. Such a board is generally more likely to be committed to fulfilling its donor's intentions.

Of course, unless board members are chosen carefully, they may steer a grantmaker in a different direction from what the founder would have wanted. There are a number of instances in which grantmakers have departed very dramatically from their founders' principles within 10 years of their deaths. A personal connection between the founder and succeeding board members often limits professional staff and unsympathetic trustees from straying too far from a donor's values—but it is not infallible.

Many donors are drawn to the idea of sunsetting because limited-life entities can spend more aggressively, over a shorter, more focused period of time. The more intense pace of grantmaking makes for an outsized spending profile, with annual giving that can be greater than that of larger, perpetual entities that limit their annual payout to the legal minimum in order to preserve endowment. Limited-life grantmaking entities thus tend to have greater philanthropic impact within their prescribed lifetimes.

Consider the John M. Olin Foundation, which exercised outsized influence in the realm of advancing conservative ideas in the latter quarter of the 20th century. Some experts attribute its effectiveness to its being a limited-lifespan foundation, sunsetting 52 years after it was founded. Even though the foundation's assets totaled not much more than $150 million, during the years it existed Olin had a spending profile of a perpetual foundation with assets of $400–500 million. The Olin Foundation made a deliberate decision to have a profound impact on its time, rather than a lighter one that spanned years into the future.

Perhaps just as importantly, limiting the life of a philanthropic entity tends to produce a greater sense of focus and purpose. Of course, sunsetting in itself does not guarantee that giving will be effective. But the knowledge that a deadline was looming certainly forced the Olin Foundation to act in ways it may not have were it a perpetual entity. Deadlines enforce discipline.

Sunsetting nevertheless presents a unique set of challenges. For example, precisely when a limited-lifespan entity should close up is debatable. Limited-life foundations often intend to spend down within 30 years of the death of the founder, or, frequently, the latter of either the founder or spouse. Some donors create a window of five years. Others have instituted 50-year lifespans. Still others have chosen not to set a fixed time period, but instead mandated a minimum annual payout percentage that is intended to run down principal over time.

There is no set rule regarding when to sunset your foundation; it depends on what the foundation is trying to accomplish. In choosing a closing date, however, your aim should be to find a happy medium between achieving your philanthropic goals and curtailing the deleterious effects that the passage of time may have on your intentions.

Finally, donors considering sunsetting should bear in mind a special problem facing limited-life entities. How should they prepare their favorite grantees—those whose missions neatly align with the vision of the grantmaker's founder—for the loss of funding that will occur when the foundation spends down? How should they plan to structure their investment portfolio in order to maintain a consistent level of support for grantees? How should they plan to retain key employees in an organization that is slated to shutter its doors? Once the close-out date is reached, what should be done with archival materials, legal documents, and any residual assets?

Again, there is no one-size-fits-all answer to these questions; much depends on the unique circumstances of the funding arrangement. Any donor considering a limited-life grantmaking entity should think about offering guidance to his successors on all of these issues.

Creating a Perpetual Entity

Finally, donors have the option of creating a grantmaking entity that will survive them into the indefinite future. Perpetuity is the most common choice among the founders of grantmaking entities. While an open-ended timeframe complicates plans for maintaining donor intent, it can also offer some advantages. For example, a perpetual grantmaking entity may be an attractive vehicle for a donor whose principal concern is providing long-term support for certain geographic regions, demographic groups, or programmatic causes. Similarly, it can make sense if a donor wants to make a certain kind of grant (like capital grants) or fund a certain activity (like supporting the arts, substance abuse, or disaster relief) where needs are likely to last forever.

Perpetuity nevertheless poses special challenges for those concerned with securing donor intent. Despite the susceptibility of perpetual entities to deviations from donor intent, there are steps that you can take to help safeguard against the corrosion of your philanthropic purposes. Some donors have employed strategies such as:

- incorporating mission statements and other donor intent documents into their bylaws and articles of incorporation;
- requiring their trustees to sign donor intent statements or to read their mission statement at every meeting of their board of directors;

- including in their founding documents a requirement for regular outside donor intent audits;
- giving outside entities legal standing to take action against the board should it stray from their mission.
- All of these practices will be explored in greater detail in later chapters.

Perpetuity is notably popular among donors creating family foundations. According to one recent study, 63 percent of family foundations are established in perpetuity, with another 25 percent considering the option of perpetuity. The same study found that the "vast majority of perpetual foundations (77 percent) have never considered options other than perpetuity." Perpetuity is often the default option for estate planners. For some founding benefactors, perpetuity is chosen somewhat unintentionally.

The same study found that one of the two most frequently given reasons for the decision to create an entity in perpetuity is the "desire for family engagement in philanthropy across generations." It is understandable why many donors hope to use a perpetual foundation in order to unify and preserve their families. Unfortunately, the record on preserving donor intent in perpetual family foundations is mixed. Money, even money dedicated to charitable purposes, can be an enormously destructive force within families. Many founding donors fail to foresee how disbursing the family's philanthropic assets can become a contentious problem, and one that is often complicated with the introduction of multiple marriages and half-siblings. Others perhaps overestimate the sense of familial fidelity and ancestral deference among individuals three, six, or ten generations in the future.

There are cases in which a perpetual family foundation may not be particularly problematic from the perspective of donor intent. For example, if a donor is confident that future generations will be better positioned to address future challenges, then perpetuity will probably not undermine his intent. Similarly, if his principal philanthropic objective is for his family to give generously to charity, his intent will be honored so long as the charitable assets continue to be disbursed by the family. Similarly, among families with very strong religious commitments and identities, donors often have great confidence that their families will remain committed to a set of common values, and are not particularly daunted by the prospect of establishing a family foundation in perpetuity.

When Honoring Donor Intent Becomes Impossible

What happens if a donor's intent in fact becomes impossible, impracticable, or even illegal to carry out? What if, say, you create a perpetual foundation exclusively dedicated to curing cancer—and a cure is found? What then happens to the corpus of the foundation? In these rare circumstances, courts may step in and apply the legal doctrine known as *cy pres* (pronounced either "see pray" or "sigh pray").

Courts have traditionally used two doctrines—deviation and *cy pres*—to allow the modification of restricted gifts. Deviation is applied to make changes in the manner that a gift is managed or administered, while *cy pres* is applied in situations where a trustee or a charity seeks to modify the donor's purpose. *Cy pres*, as commonly understood, means "as near as possible" (a rough translation of the ancient Norman phrase, *cy pres comme possible*), and it provides for the courts to modify the express terms of a charitable trust by making modifications that come as close as possible to the donor's original intent.

One of the most frequently cited examples of *cy pres* involves the bequest of the wealthy abolitionist Francis Jackson. When Jackson died in 1861, he left considerable monies in trust to fund "books, newspapers . . . speeches, lectures, and such other means as . . . will create a public sentiment that will put an end to negro slavery in this country." Four years later, at the end of the Civil War, the 13th Amendment to the Constitution

An Unavoidable Decision

If you have decided to dedicate assets to charity, you have to choose a timeframe for your giving. The decision is unavoidable. If you put it off, it will be made for you—and, quite likely, it will be perpetuity. This is not to say that the three principal approaches—spending down, sunsetting, and creating a perpetual entity— are mutually exclusive. But deciding on which of them you plan to pursue, and to what extent you plan to pursue it, should largely be determined by your charitable purpose.

ended slavery, thereby achieving the mission of Jackson's trust. The family sued to recover the funds, arguing that the purpose of the trust was now obsolete. The Massachusetts Supreme Court ruled against the family in *Jackson v. Phillips* (1867), invoking *cy pres* and directing the funds to the "use of necessitous persons of African descent in the city of Boston and its vicinity."

Another example involves John McKee, who, at the time of his death in 1902 was believed to be the wealthiest African American in the United States. McKee directed that part of his estate be held in trust until the death of his last grandchild, at which point it would be used to build "Colonel John McKee's College" for "poor colored male orphan children and poor white male orphan children." McKee left extravagant instructions for the school, down to the height and thickness of the perimeter stone wall and the parade schedule of the music and drum corps. When his last grandchild died in 1954, the trust had assets of about $1 million. While significant, the funds were nowhere near enough to fulfill his instructions. The Pennsylvania courts invoked *cy pres*, leading to the establishment of "McKee Scholarships," which continue to fund post-secondary education for fatherless young men from the greater Philadelphia area.

Today, there are three prerequisites for applying the judicial doctrine of *cy pres*: (1) the gift must be for charity; (2) the donor must have general charitable intent; and (3) the expressed purpose of a gift must be illegal, impractical, or impossible, and the charity must no longer be able to honor a donor's wishes exactly.

The greatest amount of control that you will have over your charitable giving is during your lifetime. Giving while living, however, gives you the smallest window of opportunity in which to conduct your philanthropy, and may not be the best means of addressing your long-term goals.

Creating a charitable entity that will sunset after your death gives you a bigger window of opportunity in which to give, but somewhat less control over your giving, as your directors will carry out your charitable purpose and retire your giving vehicle after your death.

Finally, a perpetual entity allows you the greatest time horizon for giving, but presents long-term challenges, and therefore requires special attentiveness, to the best way of maintaining your intent.

Carefully thinking through your charitable purpose should be the starting point for determining which of these three means of securing your charitable intent is right for you.

Additional Resources

Alliance Bernstein. *Smarter Giving for Private Foundations: A New Approach to Align Spending Policy with Mission.* September 2010.

Atlantic Philanthropies. *Turning Passion into Action: Giving While Living.* June 2010.

Beldon Fund. *Giving While Living: The Beldon Fund Spend-out Story.* March 2009.

Foundation Center. *Perpetuity or Limited Lifespan: How Do Family Foundations Decide?* April 2009.

Ostrower, Francie. *Limited Life Foundations: Motivations, Experiences, and Strategies.* Urban Institute. Center on Nonprofits and Philanthropy. February 2009.

Thelin, John R. and Richard W. Trollinger. *Time Is of the Essence: Foundations and the Policies of Limited Life and Endowment Spend-down.* Aspen Institute. 2009.

CHAPTER 3
Defining Your Mission

If you choose to spend down in your own lifetime, taking the time to define your mission is an excellent idea. It will help give you greater focus and clarity, sharpening your sense of what is central and what is peripheral to your giving.

If you choose to create an entity that will outlive you, however, defining your mission is *essential* to preserving your intentions. Donor intent is easily eroded when donors fail to make clear their intentions and wishes. In the absence of clarity, fidelity to donor intent will fade as the ideas and principles that animated the founder are ignored or forgotten.

Defining your mission is not primarily a legal matter, although it may ultimately have legal consequences. In most cases, standard bylaws, trust agreements, or articles of incorporation are not designed to protect your intent. What the law requires to establish your philanthropic vehicle is often not sufficient to define your intentions or ensure fidelity to your mission. Indeed, a well-defined mission is not among the minimum legal requirements necessary to obtain IRS approval—the IRS will accept as a mission a general reference to "charity." Your vision should be made more explicit through a mission statement (or other legacy documents) that is incorporated into your legal entity.

Defining your mission is an important step in institutionalizing your intentions so that others can, during your lifetime or in your absence, make them operational. When you are gone, the interpretation of your mission will be left to family members, trustees, and, as a last resort, the courts. The better you define your philanthropic mission during your lifetime, the better they will be able to preserve your intentions when you are gone.

Defining your mission can be a time-consuming process—it certainly takes longer than establishing the legal framework of the giving entity. Some philanthropists arrive at a clear mission only after much trial and error in making grants. Others have a clear sense of what they want to do and how they want to do it from the very beginning. Yet even in the latter case, trying to make one's intentions operational can be very challenging. Defining a mission is a deliberative process, and achieving success often requires multiple revisions.

Thinking about Your Mission Statement

When you define your philanthropic mission, try to answer this one, crucial question: *Why?* If your successors are faced with a question about your intent, they can easily look up *what* you did and *who* you funded. A carefully crafted mission statement will help them understand *why* you did it. Your mission statement should articulate the animating principles of—the reasons behind—your philanthropy. It should describe the ideas that animate your charitable purpose: the books, people, and institutions that shaped the thinking behind your giving.

As circumstances change, a mission statement that clearly describes your philosophy of giving will help to safeguard your intentions better than any list of rules or grantees ever could. It will guide those charged with carrying out your philanthropy by helping them to answer the question: What would our founder have done in these circumstances?

The result of a desultory or weak mission statement may be a sluggish or ineffective foundation with a floundering sense of purpose. It may lead to intergenerational contentiousness, altering your charitable entity into something you would not recognize or support. It can also result in legal action where courts thwart your wishes outright. Indeed, in terms of donor intent, a well-thought-out and well-written mission statement is absolutely essential for sustaining successor education, grantmaking vitality, quality control, and productive collaboration and continuity of vision among future trustees and family members. It is vital to maintaining your intentions.

Writing Your Mission Statement

Your mission statement should explain, at minimum, your reasons for establishing a foundation. A more comprehensive—and useful—mission statement will describe the principles and beliefs that inspire and guide your giving. Likewise helpful for future trustees is a statement of preferred operating principles, grantmaking guidelines, and a consideration of how succeeding generations should perpetuate your philanthropy.

Getting your mission statement right may take some trial and error. The following exercises can help you compose a mission statement that embodies and effectively communicates your intent.

Describing your values

Describing your values simply means explaining the things that are important to you and that ought to be taken into consideration by those who will be carrying out your philanthropic mission.

- Are you religious? Do you want your faith to be reflected in your philanthropy? If so, how?
- What are the ideas, traditions, persons, events, and circumstances that shaped you as a person?
- Why are you establishing a philanthropic entity? What are your motivations?

- What would be the worst thing that could happen to the assets you've dedicated to charity?
- What good are you trying to achieve? What problems are you hoping to address? Are you working to improve society in general, a certain segment of society, or an institution in a particular way?
- How important is family involvement to you?
- Over time your values may come into conflict with each other, with your heirs, or with society's changing mores. How ought such matters to be resolved?
- What parts of your foundation's mission and grantmaking would you like to remain constant over time? What aspects are nonnegotiable?

Clarifying your language

What may seem obvious to you may not be obvious to others. When you sit down to write your mission statement, don't take shortcuts. Ambiguous terms need to be carefully defined. Explain how you see the connections between your principles. Always try to put yourself in the position of a reader who has never met you. Would this person understand what you were hoping to accomplish? Would he or she have a clear picture of what motivated you? Would he or she have a good sense of the kinds of things you would want to support?

Take, for example, the late Dan Searle, former CEO of Searle Pharmaceuticals and benefactor of the Searle Freedom Trust. For six months, Searle worked closely to refine his mission statement with a trusted advisor, Kimberly O. Dennis. "I would sometimes write him notes asking him to clarify certain things," recalls Dennis. "In his notes he often referred to the importance of individual responsibility as a corollary of individual freedom. If you were going to have a free society, he would say, you needed to have personal responsibility. I wanted him to clarify what role he thought government should have in enforcing the kinds of moral values that he considered integral to personal responsibility. As it turned out, Dan thought government had no place telling people how to live their lives. But I don't think this would have come through if I hadn't asked him to clarify his thinking, because it was obvious to him but it wasn't obvious to me."

"Dan went through the mission statement, paragraphs were added, paragraphs were deleted, sentences were massaged," adds Dennis. "There is not a word in that document that Dan didn't have there very intentionally. We had long discussions over whether we should use the word *freedom* or *liberty*, over whether America is a *democracy* or a *democratic republic*. Every single word is intentional."

Formulating operating principles

In defining your mission, it is worth thinking about the principles that will guide the operation of your entity. This should not be a step-by-step set of instructions on day-to-day operations. Your aim is to describe the general contours, not to offer minute operational details.

- Do you want to support direct services to individuals: scholarships, medical care, food banks, and the like? Or do you want to effect change through advocacy and public education: policy work, research, publications? Are you comfortable with some mixture of both? If so, which do you prefer?
- Would you prefer to support local, regional, or national organizations?
- Do you prefer supporting small organizations? Start-ups? Well-established nonprofits?
- Would you rather that your funding be focused on several large grants or on many smaller grants?
- Do you prefer multi-year grants, start-up grants, or matching grants?
- What kind of relationship do you want with grantees? Do you want to give your grantees active guidance and direction? Or do you prefer to support them from a distance?
- How do you feel about supporting endowments, capital campaigns, or annual galas?
- Will you only fund specific programs? Or are you more comfortable making general-operations grants?
- What are your views on collaborative funding? Public-private partnerships?
- What kind of visibility would you like? Should your entity ever give anonymously? If so, under what circumstances? Should your successors produce an annual report, maintain a website, or otherwise promote your philanthropy?
- What is your timeframe in looking for results? Are you looking for immediate payoffs, or do you prefer to invest for the long term?
- Do you have a general sense of what kind of evaluation and assessment you would like to see in your grantmaking? Or is this the kind of question that you would rather leave to your successors? If so, you may want to make that explicit.
- Do you have strong feelings about how your assets will be invested? What do you think about mission-related investing? Program-related investing?

It may be helpful to look at other organizations that you admire. How do they operate? What do they do that makes them successful? How do they measure success?

Meeting with interested parties

By its very nature, philanthropy involves other people—giving money away implies that you're giving money away *to other people*. Your giving probably involves family members, professional colleagues, community leaders, and grant recipients. As you begin to define your mission, it is important to draw in those who will immediately be charged with helping you to execute your charitable giving: staff, trustees, family members. This might involve formal meetings with a facilitator, or a series of informal gatherings over a number of months. While the mission statement should ultimately reflect your values, talking with those who will carry out your intentions early on will help to ensure that they understand your mission.

Also consider sharing your mission statement with friends, colleagues, and interested parties. Ask for their comments. One philanthropist who left nine-figure wealth to a term-limited foundation did precisely that. "Once we had a document that he was comfortable with," says the trust's current president, "he sent it out to about two dozen people in the foundation world and the policy world. We asked for their reactions to it. People wrote long responses, sometimes several pages long. A lot of people said he should elaborate on some point, but for every person who said to elaborate, we had someone else say the material should be shortened. We incorporated some of the recommendations, but not a lot. He was persuaded by very few of them. But what the process did was give him confidence in the document we had. He found that he liked it the way it was."

Supplementing Your Mission Statement

Some foundations have developed documents intended to assist in preserving their founder's intentions that go well beyond a detailed mission statement. They create legacy statements, videos, and other collateral material intended to convey the character, passions, goals, and ideas of their founder to future generations.

The Daniels Fund has assets of over $1 billion derived from Bill Daniels' pioneering work in cable television. Daniels took great interest in his philanthropy during his lifetime and even put considerable effort into memorializing his intentions. Although Daniels created specific allocations for spending in four states and the funding areas for his foundation, he did not specify grantmaking strategies. In the absence of close involvement from his board in developing specific grantmaking strategies, staff members (who did not know Daniels or share his values) began to define the foundation's grantmaking approach.

In response, the Daniels Fund board embarked on a major five-year effort to instill Bill Daniels' values and principles in the way the foundation conducted its business. Directors pored over their founder's letters and writings. They carefully studied his giving history—he had made charitable gifts for 25 years prior to his death, nearly all of which were accompanied by a note explaining his purposes—and interviewed numerous associates to better understand his intentions. After careful consideration and deliberation, the directors defined grant areas, guidelines, and grantmaking parameters, all anchored in Daniels' words and deeds. They amended the foundation's bylaws to include these new donor-intent documents as attachments and required a 90 percent majority of the board to amend them.

The directors also assembled a wealth of supplementary material that would help to institutionalize Daniels' intentions at his foundation as well as at the major charities that he supported. They created, for example, a searchable archive of media coverage, photos, and other documents that record their founder's values, beliefs, and personal charitable contributions. And they created display cases and timelines that physically communicate Daniels' values and intentions. Interactive kiosks that explain the life and principles of Bill Daniels are located in the foundation's lobby, as well as at organizations whose histories were shaped in large part by Daniels. These items are also available to the public through the foundation's website. The sum total of these many parts is a strong statement of its benefactor's charitable mission.

Other foundations have created videos of their founder speaking candidly to a sympathetic interviewer about his or her values, principles, background, and vision. Legacy statements, which are simply a more comprehensive mission statement, have also been used to transmit donors' sensibilities across time to directors, staff, and family. Such documentation helps to capture your personal history as well as the nuance and richness of your intentions. These materials can be a powerful resource for preserving your intentions.

What a Great Mission Statement Can—and Cannot—Do

Many perpetual entities have been established in the past with vague, inconsistent, or nonexistent missions. Memorializing your philanthropic intentions through a mission statement, legacy statement, and other written or video recorded directives will not absolutely safeguard your philanthropic entity from incursions against your intentions. What it *will* do is to give those who are committed to carrying out your philanthropic intent—whether a family member, director, court, or beneficiary—a clear statement of that intent. It will give those who are inclined to preserve and advance your purposes the opportunity to do so.

CHAPTER 4
Finding the Right Vehicle(s) for Your Mission

The right charitable vehicle for your philanthropy depends on your goals and charitable objectives. Each giving entity offers you a different level of control and varying levels of responsibilities with regard to the distribution, management, and investment of your assets. And some charitable vehicles will support your philanthropic objectives and mission better than others. By matching the appropriate giving vehicle to your philanthropic mission, you will improve your chances of achieving your objectives and, over time, preserving your intentions.

This is not an either/or choice. Many donors use more than one charitable vehicle to further their philanthropic objectives. Aside from your mission and objectives, you should also take into account your estate- and tax-planning goals. The right giving entity for your philanthropic mission also hinges, to varying degrees, on whether or not you wish to establish your entity for a predetermined period of time or in perpetuity. Whether or not family members will play a role in your philanthropic legacy is another important consideration.

Charitable vehicles differ in the level of protection they afford your intentions. That is, they vary in how they can be structured, and some structures are more conducive to protecting donor intent than others. In general, however, the greater level of flexibility afforded by the charitable vehicle and the longer its lifetime, the greater possibility that donor intent may someday be compromised.

Private Foundations

The most widely established charitable vehicle is the private, non-operating foundation. (Private foundations are "non-operating" when they primarily make grants to charities rather than run their own programs.) Non-operating foundations include well-known grantmakers like the Rockefeller Foundation, the Ford Foundation, and the Bill and Melinda Gates Foundation. They also include small family foundations and large corporate foundations.

Private foundations are non-governmental, not-for-profit organizations. They are subject to federal and state laws intended to assure that they serve charitable purposes. These rules include an annual distribution requirement (5 percent of the value of its assets), an excise tax on investment income, limits on the percentage of a for-profit enterprise they may own, prohibitions forbidding self-dealing, and restrictions on grantmaking for certain kinds of recipients and activities.

Private foundations typically derive their principal funds from a single source, such as an individual, family, or corporation. These funds are governed and managed by the foundations' trustees or directors in accordance with the foundation's bylaws, trust agreement, or articles of incorporation, as well as with the laws governing charitable organizations in the state in which they are located.

Private foundations enjoy a great degree of autonomy. You can structure them to carry out your charitable mission precisely as you wish, or, at the very least, with relatively little government interference. Unfortunately, that same autonomy can also undermine your charitable intentions over time. Donors who establish private foundations with specific charitable missions must take steps at their foundation's inception to help ensure that their intentions will be honored for the life of their foundation.

Most private foundations are set up to operate in perpetuity, but donors can limit the lifespan of their entity. Most foundations make annual grant allotments to tax-exempt public charities from the investment income derived from their endowments (though some private, non-operating foundations, like corporate foundations, act more like pass-through entities, distributing the funds that the foundation receives each year from its associated company rather than building up an endowment over time).

One advantage of foundations is their ability to hire staff to make philanthropic decisions and administer grants. The flip side of this flexibility is that foundations sometimes have higher cost structures than other forms of giving. Depending on the size of a foundation, it may need financial advisors to manage assets, staff to evaluate grant applications and administer distributions, and accountants to help the foundation comply with regulations and to file annual reporting documents. The IRS has substantial reporting and paperwork requirements for foundations, and some states, like California, also require annual audits. There are, however, a growing number of companies offering low-cost administrative services to private foundations.

Donor intent

Private foundations afford donors a great deal of control. As a donor to a private foundation, you can retain nearly complete control over the management and investment of the assets contributed to your foundation. You can decide which organizations will receive contributions, and when to make distributions. During your lifetime, you can select your trustees, hire your own staff, and define geographical, philosophical, and religious limitations. You can choose to maintain a family line of directors in perpetuity, if you wish. With a private foundation, you can take steps to institutionalize your intentions and mission in a manner that will help to preserve your intentions over time.

There are other advantages to independent foundations particular to families that bear on donor intent. By their very nature, and due to the level of control they allow donors, independent foundations can memorialize a family's philanthropy. They can clarify and articulate deeply held family values and principles, involving family members over many generations and allowing them to engage actively in programs and grantmaking. A private foundation also allows the family to take greater risks in investing and to implement a long-term investment philosophy. If establishing a family philanthropic legacy is your intention, a private non-operating foundation may be the surest vehicle for securing that goal.

Structuring for donor intent

There are two principal options for structuring a private foundation: a non-stock corporation or a charitable trust. (Your charitable entity's tax-exempt status is *not* contingent on which of these you choose. Tax-exemption derives from the expenditure of funds for charitable purposes.) Each structure has advantages and disadvantages that bear directly upon donor intent. Which structure is right for your charitable entity depends upon your tolerance for change and your desire for flexibility.

In general, a charitable trust is more restrictive, limiting the activities of the foundation to those things enumerated in the trust instrument. In theory, this gives trustees little room to stray from your intentions. Formal departures from the terms of a trust can usually be made only through a petition to an appropriate court, and the attorney general in the state where the trust is established is usually a party to such proceedings.

Trustees, therefore, generally must convince both a court and an attorney general when seeking changes to the original terms of the trust. Changes are generally not permitted unless the original purpose of the trust is judged to be either impossible or impracticable. In these cases, the courts may invoke the *cy pres* doctrine to devise a course of action that comes *as close as possible* to the trust's original charitable purpose. Courts and attorneys general may vary, of course, in the strictness with which they apply the doctrine.

A charitable trust integrates your intentions in a legal structure that is—at least in theory—difficult to change. While a charitable trust structure generally offers the best protection against breaches of donor intent, it is not a fail-safe mechanism. Within the last 50 years, serious violations of donor intent have occurred within charitable trusts as well as corporations. Whichever charitable vehicle you ultimately choose, whether corporation or trust, it will not in itself be sufficient to safeguard your charitable intentions over time. Remember: it is necessary to think carefully about choosing the vehicle (or vehicles) through which your giving will be conducted. But it is not sufficient.

Establishing a private foundation as a corporation offers greater flexibility. It is a more desirable structure for donors who intend for their foundations to have employees, contracts, leases, and so forth. It may also make sense for donors who would like future directors to chart the course of their foundation. With a corporation, the foundation's charter or bylaws may be amended more easily—sometimes by a simple majority of board members.

A corporate structure retains the powers given it by state statute, and these can vary from state to state. Moreover, state legislation can affect a corporation's activities with new legislation. The California Nonprofit Integrity Act of 2004, for example, adopted new governance rules for nonprofits, including requirements for annual financial audits for foundations. Finally, in most jurisdictions it is not particularly difficult for directors to amend articles of incorporation or bylaws in ways that do not conform with the terms of the original governing documents or the intentions of their founder. This kind of flexibility, inherent in the corporation structure, can be detrimental to donor intent.

Establishing a corporate structure with members who elect directors—as opposed to simply having directors who are self-perpetuating—is one way of reducing flexibility while retaining the corporate configuration. Within this structure, members are somewhat analogous to shareholders in a for-profit corporation, in that they can elect (and remove) members of the board, but they are not necessarily on the board themselves. Members are typically fewer in number than directors, and they are appointed by the founding member, typically the donor, during his lifetime. The Arthur N. Rupe Foundation in Santa Barbara, California, is one example of a private, non-operating foundation that has a member corporate structure.

At the Rupe Foundation, the founding member, Arthur N. Rupe, may appoint or remove any of the other members. To date, he has appointed members who share his philosophical vision and who act as a safeguard for his intentions. Once Rupe is no longer capable of appointing members, the members will either become self-sustaining or the membership structure will dissolve. Thus, the membership structure can be especially useful to donors who want to retain control over their foundation during their lifetimes. Not all jurisdictions, however, have statutory provisions that allow for member nonprofit corporations.

Finally, some donors have taken additional steps to safeguard donor intent by stipulating that a percentage of their foundation's board members be made up of individuals from pre-determined third-party organizations named in the foundation's bylaws. Often these are organizations that the donor has been involved with for many years. They share the donor's philosophical outlook and act as a "watchdog" to ensure that his intentions are being carried out by the board. Other donors have given legal standing to third-party organizations that allows them to bring action against the foundation if it strays from donor intent. Still others have stipulated that regular donor-intent reviews be carried out by third parties—with real consequences for the foundation's leadership if donor intent is found to have been violated. Finally, some foundations' bylaws grant outside organizations the power to appoint the foundation's directors. The strengths and weaknesses of these strategies in preserving donor intent are considered in greater detail in Chapter 7.

Domicile

Laws governing trusts and not-for-profit corporations vary from state to state. Choosing a home for your foundation can be an important decision regarding donor intent. Delaware, for example, has a notably expedient court system, flexible corporate laws, and a renowned position as a corporate and financial center, making the state an attractive legal home for private foundations regardless of their philanthropic focus. In fact, Delaware is the legal home to many foundations that fund exclusively in states far from Delaware. Likewise, Florida, Virginia, and Texas have enacted provisions into law that support philanthropic freedom and that restrict the state from attempting to direct foundations' charitable missions or giving.

Other important questions of state law include the scope of trustee or director indemnification; the filing requirements for operating a foundation; and provisions permitting the board to transfer the foundation into a new jurisdiction, which can allow the foundation to take advantage of another state's laws. The donor must determine whether, and how much, flexibility will be desirable. In any case, a foundation's "home state" will generally require the foundation to register with the state's charities bureau.

Operating Foundations

Some private foundations are established as, or later become, operating foundations. Private operating foundations use the majority of their revenue to provide their own charitable services and programs. They make few or no grants to outside organizations. Museums, libraries, and research facilities such as the Getty Trust and the Carnegie Endowment for International Peace are examples of operating foundations.

Liberty Fund, located in Indianapolis, is an operating foundation that was established to encourage the study of the ideal of a society of free and responsible individuals. Its founder, Pierre F. Goodrich, believed in a unique educational model for advancing the ideas that underpin a free society. He was convinced that education in a free society requires a dialogue centered in the great ideas of civilization, and he advanced this notion through focused seminars directed by scholars.

Goodrich founded Liberty Fund in 1960 to develop, supervise, and finance its own educational activities in order to foster thought and encourage discourse on enduring issues pertaining to liberty. Goodrich had to create, by establishing an operating foundation, the very organization that would carry out his intentions. He understood that operating foundations are best suited to philanthropic missions that are unique and that cannot be carried out by an existing organization.

To qualify as an operating foundation, your organization must spend at least 85 percent of its adjusted net income or its minimum investment return directly on its exempt activities—its programs. An operating foundation is not subject to minimum charitable distribution requirements. As a further benefit, contributions to private operating foundations are deductible up to 50 percent of a donor's adjusted gross income, whereas contributions to non-operating foundations are generally limited to 30 percent. Finally, a private operating foundation may receive qualifying distributions from a non-operating foundation if the non-operating foundation does not control the operating foundation.

Because private operating foundations fund, direct, and administer their own programs, they have direct control over how their funds are spent. If programs and operations stray from the foundation's philanthropic mission, they have no one to blame but themselves. In this way, operating foundations may be said to be a more satisfactory way of securing and preserving donor intent than non-operating foundations.

Operating foundations, however, are also subject to many of the same problems as a non-operating foundation, including mission creep. Nor are they immune from the deleterious effects that time can have on a donor's intentions. In other words, while an operating foundation gives you and your directors more immediate control over how your charitable funds are directed, it does not necessarily guarantee that the foundation as a whole will stay true to its mission over time.

Community Foundations

Community foundations are tax-exempt, nonprofit, autonomous, and publicly supported philanthropic institutions composed primarily of permanent funds established by many separate donors. Historically, they were established for the long-term and diverse charitable benefit of the residents of a defined geographic area. According to Foundation Center, there were 737 community foundations in 2009, the last year for which data is available.

The Columbus Foundation in Columbus, Ohio, for example, was established in 1943 by Harrison M. Sayre and a group of concerned citizens who wanted to improve their community through charitable giving. Today, the Columbus Foundation is the ninth largest community foundation in the country, with over $1 billion in assets representing over 1,800 donors. Like other community foundations, Columbus' assets are composed of an assortment of unrestricted funds that the foundation can use to fund its own programs, like its Safety Net Fund, which helps the region's most needy citizens. It also contains funds restricted to specific charitable purposes through outright gifts or planned gifts. Columbus also manages donor-advised funds and supporting organizations. Like most community foundations, donors who make gifts through the Columbus Foundation are no longer restricted to a specific geographic area in their giving. In order to compete in an emerging philanthropic-services marketplace, most community foundations have broadened their giving missions and donor services.

Donor intent

Community foundations allow expression of individual philanthropy in a public charity setting. When you choose to donate to a community foundation, you have a number of options.

- *First*, you may give to a general unrestricted fund, which allows the foundation the most flexibility to respond to community needs and to fund its own programs. This gives you the least control over how your charitable gift will be directed.
- *Second*, you can set up a designated fund, which allows you to retain some control over the ultimate use of your philanthropic dollars. Many community foundations, for example, allow donors to establish scholarship funds designated for the benefit of particular schools.
- *Third*, you can create a donor-advised fund, which affords you more, but not ultimate, control over where your charitable dollars will be directed.

Several other types of designated funds at community foundations allow donors to have limited control over the recipients of their philanthropy, including field-of-interest funds, scholarship funds, and restricted funds. In each case, you can broadly designate where and when the money ought to go.

It is important to recognize, however, that most gifts to community foundations are precisely that: gifts that you no longer control. Even with designated funds, the community foundation frequently maintains flexibility for grantmaking within broadly defined and predetermined categories. Most funds are ultimately owned and controlled by the foundation. Some donor-directed funds revert to the community foundation's general unrestricted fund after a period of time or after the death of the donor. Grantmaking activities are usually overseen by a governing or distribution board that is supposed to be representative of various community interests.

With community foundation donor-advised funds, you can reasonably expect to exercise informal influence over the distribution and investment of your funds. Nevertheless, even donor-advised funds are no longer *your* funds once you have gifted them. They belong to the community foundation. You may advise but you cannot control.

Historically, community foundations were the only option for donors who wanted to support their local community but who did not have the assets, time, or interest to establish their own charitable entity. As competition for philanthropic services has increased, however, donors now have many more options.

Some donors remain wary of community foundations because of their discretionary philanthropy. Many community foundations, for example, quietly refrained from making grants from their discretionary funds to the Boy Scouts because of its policy on homosexual adult leaders. Gifts to family-planning organizations and polarizing community activist groups have also alienated many donors from their local community foundations. For these donors, the philosophical outlook of their local community foundation simply does not match their own. Needless to say, if your funds are ultimately controlled by an organization that does not share your philosophical and philanthropic outlook, there is little chance that your intentions will be preserved over time.

Mission-driven Intermediaries

Public charity organizations that function like community foundations but that are mission driven and have a national reach have emerged in recent decades. These organizations offer the kind of philanthropic investment advice and giving vehicles found in community foundations. But instead of a geographic region, they are organized to support a specific cause or point of view.

For example, DonorsTrust, based in Alexandria, Virginia, is philosophically committed to the ideals of limited government, personal responsibility, and free enterprise. It was founded in response to charitable organizations—like many community foundations—that don't always share the same principles as their donors, potentially creating conflict over donor intent. Other mission-driven public charities also work with like-minded donors who share their approach to giving. Funders interested in supporting left-of-center nonprofits, for example, can work with the Tides Foundation. Similarly, there are scores of mission-driven public charity intermediaries for Catholic, evangelical, and Jewish donors.

What mission-driven charities offer you in structuring your philanthropic entity is the opportunity to create your philanthropy with like-minded people. Such groups often prove to be good stewards of your philanthropic legacy because they share your philosophical values.

Donor-advised Funds

Donor-advised funds originated within community foundations as a way for donors to establish a relatively small individual fund and to designate their fund's recipients. Donors receive tax deductions for their contributions and at the same time give up formal control of its investment or distribution. Donor-advised fund services are increasingly being offered by other types of public charities (like Rotary International and World Vision), federated giving programs (like United Way), universities, and other charitable institutions. There are also commercial donor-advised funds, which have greatly expanded since Fidelity launched its Charitable Gift Fund in 1992.

The principal advantage of donor-advised funds is their simplicity. They have relatively few rules and restrictions, and the tax benefits are immediate, even though distributions can be deferred for many years. Gifts of cash are tax-deductible up to 50 percent of adjusted gross income, and they are not subject to the excise tax or to an annual payout requirement. Nevertheless, donor-advised funds typically have high payout rates, usually about 15 percent.

Organizations that host your fund can also accept gifts such as art, land, and business assets with significant tax benefits. Much of the costly administrative work associated with any philanthropic initiative—such as processing applications, philanthropic planning, as well as tax, legal, and accounting services—is carried out by the host organization. A donor-advised fund can be established online or over the telephone. In sum, the cost of a donor-advised fund is often considerably lower than the cost of operating and administering a private foundation.

It is also worth noting that an account at a donor-advised fund cannot be used to fund your administrative staff, foundation expenses, or family office. (Unlike a private non-operating foundation, donor-advised fund expenditures can only be made to qualified nonprofit entities, not to operating expenses.) In some cases, a donor-advised fund provider may be willing to hire a philanthropic consultant to assist with gift planning and pay the consultant from its general operating funds. (In return, the provider would likely charge the account additional administrative fees to defray the direct and indirect costs of hiring a consultant.) Of course, an individual establishing a donor-advised fund account could, at his own expense, hire staff to assist him with his charitable giving.

Donor anonymity is an especially important benefit of donor-advised funds. Because your gift is made to the host organization, distributions from your fund can remain anonymous, if you choose. This is an important factor for individuals who do not want to be inundated with solicitations or have their giving history made public through annual IRS filings, or who simply want to keep their charitable giving anonymous.

Donor intent

While donor advised funds do offer convenience and anonymity, it is important to understand that once you have made a contribution to a donor-advised fund, those funds no longer belong to you. Regulations mandate that your charitable contribution must be irrevocable and unconditional in order for you to receive the associated tax benefits. You cannot, for example, use your donor-advised fund to pay off a personal pledge. Furthermore, donor-advised funds cannot contain material restrictions or conditions that would limit the autonomy of the host organization over the fund. The host organization legally retains final discretion on where to donate.

The independent discretion of a donor-advised fund carries important implications for donor intent. While in practice the donor's wishes are *usually* followed—that is only good for business, after all—host organizations can and sometimes do reject the donor's recommendations. On the one hand, host organizations need their clients to feel as if they are in control of their donor-advised fund, in order to maintain good customer relations and grow their portfolio. On the other hand, federal regulations require host organizations to prove that you are in fact *not* in control of the fund.

To help secure their intent, individuals using donor-advised funds should have contingency plans in place in case their funds retain significant assets at the time of their death. For example, there should be a named successor advisor. The principles that govern the selection of board members are applicable to the selection of a successor advisor. (For further information on choosing board members, please see Chapter 5.) Similarly, it is worth considering a sunset clause for assets still held in donor-advised funds.

A final word of caution: because of their relative newness and rapid growth, donor-advised funds have been subject to increasing regulatory scrutiny. Lawmakers have considered from time-to-time whether or not the funds should be subject to minimum distributions and an excise tax on investment earnings, similar to private, non-operating foundations. Regulatory changes in this realm could adversely affect your charitable intentions.

Supporting Organizations

A supporting organization is a distinct legal entity that has a supporting relationship with a public charity. Because of this supporting relationship, it qualifies as a public charity rather than a private foundation even though it may have only one donor or one family of donors. It is one of the few organizations that has public-charity status for tax deductibility but is not required to meet the public-support test (that is, it does not need to receive at least one-third of its support from the general public).

Although a supporting organization may be formed to benefit any type of public charity, the use of this form is particularly common in connection with community foundations, university endowment funds, and organizations that provide essential services for hospital systems. Supporting organizations can save donors from the paperwork, administrative, and reporting responsibilities associated with a private foundation. Also, generations of family members may act as advisors to the organization—whose board can comprise at least some donor-chosen members—and retain control over the choice of grantees, the timing of distributions, and investment policies.

Contributions to a supporting organization qualify for more favorable tax advantages than those used to establish a private foundation. Also, supporting organizations are not subject to minimum annual distribution requirements. The day-to-day operations of a supporting organization are typically handled by the supported organization, which is attractive to donors who do not want to be involved in the administrative duties, grant management, and IRS filings. Along with these advantages, however, come important drawbacks regarding control. By law, the supporting organization cannot be controlled by the donor. Establishing the supporting organization and realizing the enhanced tax advantages entails making an irrevocable gift, which you cannot control. In most cases, the supported organization will be respectful of the donor's intentions during his lifetime—they are interested in future gifts. Once the donor is no longer in a position to make future grants, however, the supported organization loses an important incentive to honor donor intent.

While a supporting organization can operate in much the same way as a private foundation, there are important ways in which it is different. To qualify as a supporting organization, a foundation must meet one of three legal tests that assure, at a minimum, that the supported charity has some significant influence over the actions of the supporting organization and that the organization is responsive to the needs of the charity. In other words, in a supporting organization scenario, the organization supported by your philanthropy must have influence over your grantmaking. If you choose this charitable entity to carry out your philanthropic mission, you should recognize that the supported organization may come to exercise considerable influence over your philanthropic intentions over time. You should also give careful consideration to securing expert counsel—supporting organizations are complicated.

Donor intent

Consider the example of the Robertson Foundation. Charles and Marie Robertson established a supporting organization in 1961 to train young Americans for careers in public service (specifically in diplomatic or international roles) at Princeton University's Woodrow Wilson School of Public and International Affairs. At the time, the Robertsons' gift of $35 million was the largest donation ever made to the university.

As a supporting organization, the Robertson Foundation was typical in that it was established primarily to support the activities of Princeton University. One of the advantages of a supporting organization is that it allows donors to be involved in decision-making regarding the investment and distribution of funds. As such, the Robertsons, and subsequent generations of family members, served on the foundation's board along with representatives from Princeton.

Over time, however, family members discerned that the university was no longer carrying out the original intent of the gift and, instead, was using the supporting organization's funds, which had swelled to over $900 million by 2007, for other, unrelated activities. Family members were outnumbered by university representatives, four to three, on the board. After making great efforts to resolve the issue, the family members sued the university in 2002, beginning a long legal battle that was finally settled in 2008, when Princeton paid approximately $100 million to the Robertsons in what has been called the largest donor-intent award in history.

The supporting organization vehicle was probably not the right vehicle to safeguard the Robertsons' intentions over time, especially after the death of the original donors. While it did give their heirs as directors standing to litigate, the nature of the vehicle stacks the cards against the preservation of donor intent. That is, a supporting organization must at minimum share authority with the *supported* organization. Over time, the interests of the supported organization may very well come into conflict with the intentions of the supporting organization and its founders.

At a more general level, there may be strategies donors can use to protect their intent in establishing a supporting organization. If a donor has allies within the supported organization—a trusted faculty member, for example, or perhaps a close associate on the board of the organization—he can ask that those individuals be appointed to the board of the supporting organization, thus filling the slots reserved for representatives of the supported organization with people who are likely to be sympathetic to the donor's wishes. Another fallback strategy may involve including an exit clause providing for the funds to go to an alternative organization, in the event that the supporting organization finds itself unable to carry out the donor's instructions.

Different Vehicles, Different Purposes

For many donors, the choice of a giving vehicle is not an either/or question. A family may have a family foundation, a number of charitable trusts, and several donor-advised funds, each with its own purpose and strategy. Today, donor-advised funds are regarded less as alternatives to other giving vehicles and more as potential complements to a family's other charitable entities. In choosing the right giving vehicle for your philanthropic mission, it is important to match and structure each vehicle according to the charitable goals and objectives you wish it to serve. It is important for you to consider what values you would like your philanthropic dollars to advance, and to choose the giving vehicle or mix of giving vehicles most likely to accomplish your goals.

CHAPTER 5
Naming Your Board

Philanthropy is a deeply human undertaking. If you are leaving money to others to disburse to charity, you are charging them with an enormous trust. Choose the right people and you will be well-positioned to see your mission properly executed. But choose the wrong people and there is no legal framework or checks and balances that can safeguard your intentions. Taking time to carefully think through the selection of your board members—and, crucially, how they will perpetuate themselves once you are gone—is critical to preserving your mission. In fact, choosing board members may be the most important decision you make.

For this reason, there is more to choosing good board members than bringing aboard your lawyer, golf buddy, and son-in-law. You cannot simply apply the best practices of human resource management. Family members are equally tricky. It is tempting to hope that your kids will come to see things your way, or that the sharp differences between them will work themselves out once they find themselves seated around a boardroom. To be sure, expertise and family ties have their place in your decision. But neither should be your primary consideration when choosing the people you will entrust with your philanthropic resources.

Cultivating Board Members
There is, of course, no tidy way of determining another person's character or predicting how someone will behave in your absence. If there were, the matter of preserving donor intent would be easy. Nor are there fixed rules that, if you follow to the letter, will produce the same result every time. Choosing good board members is really a matter of cultivation and discernment, more an art than a science.

To cultivate board members means getting to know them. It means discussing over a long period of time their thinking, especially their thinking about the nature of philanthropy. It means posing questions that will uncover areas of agreement—and, equally importantly, disagreement. Do not settle for "yes" or "no" answers. Asking tough questions now may preserve the intent of your foundation in later years.

You will be best positioned to choose trustees if you watch how they perform on the job. When the first generation of a board worked directly with the benefactor, it generally does a better job of perpetuating his intentions. The give-and-take of making grants with those who will survive you and perpetuate your legacy will help you to assess their individual ability to serve as successors. They will also benefit from working with you during your lifetime, learning, as you

Donor Intent Is a Moral Concern

When considering the men and women who will govern and run your foundation, the most important thing in preserving your intentions over time is their moral character and philosophical outlook. Considerably less important is whether or not they are business associates, family members, or philanthropic-sector professionals. Proficiency in the law, program areas, or foundation management may be helpful in myriad ways when it comes to setting up and operating your foundation. But safeguarding your intentions is another matter. Whether or not a trustee will earn the faith you have put in him is, at heart, a *moral* rather than a *technical* problem.

Perpetuating your intent after you are gone makes moral demands of your trustees. They must be humble enough to subordinate their interests and enthusiasms to the mission you set for them. They must be disciplined enough to constantly revisit and re-engage your vision. And they must be brave enough to take managerial, fiduciary, or legal steps to protect your intent when they feel it has been compromised.

Make character and philosophical outlook your primary considerations when choosing trustees. Most people can be taught how to serve on a board relatively quickly. The willingness to subordinate one's own desires in the service of another, however, is a matter of character, one that is often developed over a lifetime.

express your giving preferences and put your mission into action, how precisely your grantmaking fulfills your goals.

Board members who share your philosophical and philanthropic outlook will also help you to define and refine your giving. In most cases, a donor begins his foundation with a certain idea, and that idea evolves over time through the successes and failures of grantmaking. Involving the individuals who will survive you in the development of the decision-making life of your grantmaking entity while you are alive is instrumental to upholding your intentions when you are gone. It can also be an especially effective way for helping family members to understand your philanthropic goals. They will learn from you—and you from them.

In speaking candidly with your trustees about first principles and donor intent, you may or may not discover in a granddaughter or a long-time legal counsel someone who shares your point of view. Will you find through grantmaking the board members who will stand up for the principles upon which you established your foundation? Whether or not you do, your legacy will be better preserved for having cultivated board members who share your outlook.

Populating Your Board

Remember: you are putting together a board. This will be a group of people, and group dynamics will come into play. These people will have to work together. Think about how they will interact with one another. How well do any of these individuals know each other? Are they friends, colleagues, acquaintances, or strangers? How do these individuals relate to you? Do some of them know you as a personal friend, while others know you as a business associate? How different will their impressions of you be? To what degree have you been candid about your intentions with each of them? Can you foresee fault lines opening among the individuals in this group? If so, what can be done to mitigate them? Is there a particularly forceful personality who could dominate the board?

There are certain types of board members that donors should probably avoid. For instance, the ideal board member should neither be too aggressive nor too passive. An overly aggressive board member can lead to unnecessary and counter-productive friction; a too-passive board member may not be willing to stand on principle on important questions of donor intent. Similarly, board members should have neither too many nor too few competing demands on their time. Board members who cannot dedicate the time and energy to their duties may be overly reliant on others (especially staff) for setting a strategic vision; those without competing demands on their time may expand their roles beyond leadership and into staff functions.

Structuring Your Board

In addition to honoring your intent, foundation boards have other responsibilities. Their duties include managing the investment of your corpus, complying with all relevant laws and codes, and (in some cases) overseeing the performance of a professional staff.

Furthermore, your philanthropy may benefit from senior-level expertise in specific fields, such as medicine, public policy, or education reform. Expert board members can be invaluable in assessing the effectiveness and qualifications of grant recipients. The issue for some donors, then, is how to develop a board that shares their philosophical outlook and commitment to donor intent while also ensuring that it has the skill sets necessary to carry out the business of the foundation.

Some donors have approached this issue by structuring their foundations with multi-tiered boards, with separate responsibilities assigned to each tier. The Searle Freedom Trust in Washington, D.C., for example, has three distinct tiers that make up its board of directors. The first tier—the trustees—is responsible for handling the foundation's resources. This tier was directed to manage financial affairs; it allows technical experts to do their work without being involved in the foundation's grantmaking decisions.

The second tier—grant advisors—consists of four advisors, chosen by the founder, who have expertise in areas related to the foundation's grantmaking: these advisors are primarily public intellectuals with academic, public policy, and think-tank management experience. They share the donor's general philosophical outlook: a commitment to individual freedom, economic liberty, personal responsibility, and traditional American values. They worked closely with the donor during his lifetime. In some cases, the grant advisors have affiliations with organizations that the foundation has supported and built relationships with over time. The grant advisors, with the advice and assistance of the professional staff, make the actual decisions about where and how the foundation will direct its funding.

The third tier—the family advisors—consists of direct descendants of Daniel C. Searle, the founder. They are required to meet at least once annually with the grant advisors to review grants and have the power, on a unanimous basis, to overturn the decisions of the grant advisors. By design, the family advisors are a prudent check on the overall direction of the foundation. They, of course, bring a personal perspective to the board, one that is instructive in answering the question: If the founder were here today, what would he do? Family members participate in but do not control absolutely the affairs of the foundation. None of the tiers do. The strength of the tiered approach is in the way it separates board powers and responsibilities and delegates them to those best suited to perform them. The structure accentuates the unique abilities of the different tiers while encouraging enough cooperation among them that, in fact, the third tier of family advisors seldom if ever rejects the grantmaking decisions of the second-tier grant advisors.

The success of Searle's tiered board structure is a consequence of the donor's ability to find advisors who shared his philosophical outlook and who could work well together. He worked with and cultivated his family and grant advisors during his lifetime. Doing so brought clarity rather than conflict to the practical operation of the tiered structure by specifying roles and spheres of authority. Simply creating a tiered structure will not force board members who do not share your views into conformity. It may even foster resentment and power struggles. The tiered board structure is a complement, not a replacement, for cultivating individuals who share your first principles. It is meant to enhance the operations of a board that shares your goals.

There is no easy way to determine whether creating a tiered board structure is right for your entity. The path you should take is contingent, in part, on your foundation's size, mission, areas of giving, when or if you intend to sunset, and whether or not there are family members involved. Tiering, however, can be an important tool to help preserve your legacy and should be considered as you deliberate the future of your foundation.

Compensating Your Board Members

In October 2003, the *Boston Globe* reported on a number of small foundations with giant benefits. Among the *Globe's* revelations was the compensation package offered to Paul Cabot Jr. From 1998 through 2002, Cabot was paid over $5.1 million for his service as a trustee of the Paul and Virginia Cabot Charitable Trust, even though the foundation gave only about $2 million to charity during this period. The scandal grabbed headlines and re-opened the question of whether it is ever appropriate to compensate the board members of philanthropic foundations.

Throughout the controversy, little if any thought was given to how compensation might be seen in light of donor intent. That was unfortunate, since compensating board members can be another mechanism for preserving donor intent. Board compensation practices vary widely, and there are benefits and drawbacks to either practice.

Arguments in favor of board compensation

1. It can clarify the agency question. Whether they take payment of $1 or $100,000, your board members can be seen, in a moral (although not legal) sense, as working for you. Through compensation, you can make clear your expectation that board members are not to see themselves as volunteers motivated by an altruistic desire to pursue some moral good as they see fit. Rather, by compensating your board members you are underscoring the moral fact that you intend for them to act, through the organization, as your agents, paid to execute the mission you have established at your institution. If you choose to compensate for this reason, it is a good idea to make your expectations explicit, conditioning payment on your board members acknowledging, in writing, that by accepting compensation they are acting in good faith as paid agents.

2. It removes blanket immunity. The federal Volunteer Protection Act of 1997 (as well as similar statutes in many states) provides broad immunity from tort claims that might be filed against the volunteers of nonprofit organizations. As Harvey Dale of New York University has observed, uncompensated board members thus have a "lower risk of being held liable for negligence (or violation) of fiduciary duties." If you provide even minimal compensation, you will eliminate this exculpatory protection and, according to Dale, you are "likely to increase the attention directors pay to fulfilling their fiduciary duties."

3. It widens the pool of available board members. If you want specialized expertise on your board, you may have to offer some form of payment in order to secure the service of people whose time is extremely valuable. World-class experts in biomedical research, for example, may only be willing to serve on your board for a fee. Perhaps you want fellow entrepreneurs. Perhaps you want to increase diversity on your board. People have competing demands on their time. Retaining their services may very well require paying them.

Arguments against board compensation

1. It's a departure from the nonprofit tradition of volunteerism. Board members at grant-receiving public charities are generally expected to serve without compensation, while board members at grantmaking private philanthropies face no such expectation. This expectation is strong enough that many foundations would not make grants to public charities that compensated board members. If grant recipients are basically barred from paying their boards, why should grantmakers be allowed to do so?

2. It may not be necessary. You may decide that compensation simply isn't necessary to attract well-qualified board members. You may even decide that the only people you want on your board are precisely those enthusiastic enough about your mission to offer their time, free of charge.

Board compensation can be one means of harnessing individual self-interest for the purpose of preserving your intent. Whether or not it is appropriate for your foundation depends, in part, on the actual demands of board service: the time and effort that must be expended for meetings, site visits, proposal reviews, and service on committees, among other responsibilities. Recognizing the intersection between board service and self-interest will help you to think about what is appropriate for your circumstances.

Planning for Board Succession

Planning for board succession is an area where efforts to perpetuate donor intent often falter. Whether you intend to sunset your foundation or establish it in perpetuity, your founding board members in most cases will bear the responsibility of perpetuating themselves. The longer the anticipated life of your foundation, the more important it is to articulate a process for choosing the next generation of men and women who will oversee it.

"Look for These Qualities"

Bill [Daniels] said, "Here's a list of buddies that you ought to call on when you need to replace directors." I think it would have been very helpful if he had said, "When you look for future directors, look for these qualities," instead of saying, "Look for these people."

—Linda Childears
President and CEO, Daniels Fund

Board succession should unfold according to a predetermined plan, one that you have carefully considered with your original board members. The sudden loss of a key individual should not cause a crisis. If you have cultivated a set of founding board members who share your philosophic and philanthropic outlook, you have already taken one of the most important steps in ensuring that their successors will see eye-to-eye with your vision. The same qualities of character and commitment that you sought in your first-generation board members, and your process of cultivating them, ought to be emulated in choosing future generations of the board. Discussing with your founding board members and committing to paper the specific qualifications for future leadership is vitally important in transmitting your intentions.

Should you establish a foundation in perpetuity, keep in mind the importance of age diversity on your board. If the men and women whom you appoint in your lifetime as board members are of your peer group and of a similar age, it is conceivable that they may all retire at or about the same time. Imagine what would happen if there were a sudden and complete turnover of long-time board members without apparent successors. It could easily jeopardize your intent. To prevent it, try to stagger the ages of your board members.

Hiring Staff for Your Mission

It is vital that you ensure your board members' fidelity to donor intent—but those efforts could come to nothing if you ignore your staff. Unfortunately, foundation staff can easily be ideologically removed from both the organization's founder and its board. But, depending on the structure and size of your foundation, staff can have an outsized influence on how your mission is executed.

Hire the Right People

When I was hired as president and CEO of the Daniels Fund, I was stunned by how many professionals in philanthropy asked me, "What new direction will you take at the Daniels Fund?" It simply never occurred to me that I would take the Daniels Fund in any direction other than the one defined by our donor. It seems commonplace for many of my peers in the foundation world to believe that fidelity to donor intent denies them the ability to creatively respond to the "problems of today." They have the right to their opinions, but they do not have the right to violate donor intent. There is an old saying: *personnel is policy*. What it means is that it's necessary to hire staff members who are philosophically in line with your mission and who will work to achieve it. Each new staff member you hire, at any level of the organization, is a vote you are casting in favor of donor intent—or in favor of its dismantling.

—Linda Childears
President and CEO, Daniels Fund

Staff members are on the front line meeting with organizations. Every day, they make dozens of relatively small decisions. The sum of these "little" decisions determines the proposals that will ultimately appear before the board. Over time, the effect can amount to an abdication of board responsibilities to staff members. For many reasons—ranging from labor laws to the reasonable desire to avoid unpleasant employment conflict—staff members often have the upper hand on board members, even if they lack the office.

Professional staff members are as vital to preserving and perpetuating the mission of the foundation as the board members. Like board members, they should be cultivated over time, given more responsibility as they show a greater appreciation and understanding of the foundation's mission. Taking the time to know and understand the character and intellectual commitments of prospective staff members, rather than merely considering their professional qualifications, is indispensable to preserving your intentions.

The Human Touch

The affairs of foundations belong, ultimately, to the messy realm of human interactions. Developing legal and organizational safeguards is essential to preserving your intentions over time. But whether or not these structural measures amount to anything largely depends upon the character and philosophical outlook of the men and women who govern and manage your foundation. Getting to know their ethical and intellectual dispositions and nurturing them in the grantmaking habits of your foundation is an important step in preserving your intentions. In other words, the time that you invest in your first-generation board members and staff will go a long way in creating a culture of fidelity to donor intent among later generations.

CHAPTER 6
Instituting Board Policies to Reinforce Your Intent

Establishing board polices that reinforce donor intent is essential to institutionalizing your philanthropic legacy. Having defined and memorialized your mission in your philanthropy's originating documents, it is now necessary to think about how these legal documents will become functional. Legal papers that codify your charitable intentions are a necessary but, unfortunately, not sufficient step in securing your philanthropic mission. Your mission must be made operational.

How, practically speaking, will your heirs, board members, and directors come to know your intentions? What steps can be taken to ensure that these documents are not ignored, that they instead become the operational framework that guides day-to-day grantmaking? How will your intent shape the culture at the entity you create?

A culture that honors your intent begins with your board, for they are the ones who are legally and morally bound to uphold your mission as it is established in your foundational documents. Taking steps to institute policies that will assist them in understanding, defending, and implementing your intentions, especially after you are gone, will help them to secure your charitable purpose. There are numerous board policies that can be adopted—from a simple reading of bylaws and mission statement prior to each directors' meeting to annual donor-intent reviews—to help make your philanthropic intentions operational.

Reviewing Your Mission at Board Meetings

The first step in institutionalizing your mission is to ensure that those who are charged with carrying it out know and understand what it is. To this end, some foundations have adopted the practice of reading and discussing their originating documents at their annual meeting. Others do it at each and every meeting of their board of directors.

Reading the foundation's mission statement reminds directors of their founder's original purpose and, through discussion, gives them the opportunity to ask how they are measuring up to their donor's intent. Furthermore, it gives board members the proper lens through which to view the business of the foundation before them at each meeting.

You may also consider having legacy statements printed at the top of their meeting agenda or in the front of their board book. This helps to constantly remind

"Read the Entire Indenture, Out Loud, Once a Year"

Our founder, James B. Duke, required his trustees to read the entire indenture, out loud, once a year. We do it every February at our board meeting. It takes about 45 minutes, and it's a wonderful way for the board and senior management to hear his voice and to focus on his wishes.

—Eugene W. Cochrane Jr.
President, Duke Endowment

the directors of the founder's charitable purpose. Unless time is set aside in the agenda to discuss the entity's mission, however, it may go unread. Some foundations schedule a portion of each meeting, or at least each annual meeting or annual retreat, to review and discuss founding documents and other relevant materials authored by, or pertaining to, the donor, including legacy statements, interviews, or letters. Others invite past board chairs and senior family members to their meetings to discuss the grantmaking history of the foundation and its founder.

At the Daniels Fund, most of the directors have been video-recorded discussing their relationship with the founder, Bill Daniels, and how they understand his donor intent. Their bylaws require that time is set aside at each annual meeting to reflect on Daniels and his philosophy of giving, and each year a director is asked to prepare a presentation discussing Daniels' intentions. Other foundations begin each board meeting by sharing a story, correspondence, or testimonial about a grant that is manifestly advancing the foundation's mission.

The aim of these exercises goes beyond merely transmitting the *words* of the founder to current and future generations. The object is to create a *culture* that honors donor intent within the organization. When staff and grantees see that your board takes time from their busy schedule to review, to understand in light of changing circumstances, and to honor your intentions, it resonates. Such practices instill and reinforce a sense that the founder's intent should guide every important decision that the organization makes. This kind of culture *within* the organization is transmitted *outside* the organization to grantees and potential grantees. When this happens, those who seek support from your philanthropy will not waste their time, or yours, if they think that their work lies outside of your mission. In this way, securing donor intent can become a self-reinforcing activity.

Cultivating Fidelity to Your Intent

In addition to repeatedly referencing a foundation's mission at board meetings, there are other ways to encourage board members to adhere to and to honor donor intent. Recruitment, training, and evaluation of board members are junctures at which members can reflect on their ability to advance a foundation's mission.

Requiring board members to sign a statement

Your board, for example, may simply adopt a code of ethics that stipulates that members honor donor intent. Prospective board members may be required to participate in an orientation regarding the foundation's giving values, and then subscribe in writing to the foundation's mission. The Daniels Fund requires its board members to sign a Statement of Commitment and Understanding. After reviewing a detailed set of documents that describes the life, values, character, and intentions of the founder, directors are asked to sign a statement that reads, in part:

> Signing this document affirms your commitment to preserve Bill Daniels' donor intent and his personal style of conducting business (as described in this document). You agree to set aside your personal views or preferences when acting on behalf of the Daniels Fund. It is the Board's responsibility to ensure that the Daniels Fund most effectively fulfills Bill Daniels' intentions and remains true to his ideals. You also acknowledge that you have read this document and understand its importance in guiding the efforts of the Daniels Fund.

Instituting trustee apprenticeships

The Samuel Roberts Noble Foundation in Ardmore, Oklahoma, has adopted the practice of having apprentices or "advisory-trustees." These apprentices to the board attend regular trustees' meetings and receive the same compensation as other board members. They stay abreast of all the activities of the board, rotating off after a one-year period. Some—but not all—apprentice trustees go on to become actual board members. Being an advisor-trustee does not guarantee that one will become a board member. Developing a mechanism for cultivating new trustees or directors through an apprenticeship program is an excellent way to evaluate and identify new board members. Such a mechanism should be a part of any succession planning, especially for perpetual foundations.

Enacting peer review among board members

It is worth considering a process for evaluating and retaining board members based on their commitment to fulfilling your intent. One way to do so is to create a review process that assesses how the individual director respected donor intent in carrying out his duties. Other director or trustee assessments might evaluate whether the candidate is knowledgeable concerning the foundation's mission and active in carrying it out; whether the candidate devotes ample time, thought, and resources to achieve the mission; whether he has the necessary skills to meet the foundation's mission; and whether he has the necessary relationships with persons and organizations to advance the foundation's mission as the donor intended. Here it is important that your bylaws include provisions for selective turnover of board members, or at least a requirement that each member be "re-elected" to the board after a period of time. A re-election process can compel board members to reflect on their performance and the performance of others, and to be more conscientious in carrying out activities consistent with your intentions.

Creating board member removal powers

Annual reviews are not the only mechanisms, of course, for removing board members who are not faithful to your intent from your board. You might give a supermajority of the board the power to remove any individual director, or you could vest that power in a family member, a family advisor, an independent individual, or an existing entity, such as a public charity with which you wish the foundation to have a close relationship. The Roe Foundation, for example, has given the Mont Pelerin Society and the Philadelphia Society—two organizations in which founding benefactor Thomas A. Roe was involved and that share his philosophical outlook—standing to sue the foundation's board members if they depart from his intent. Be advised, however, that such "watchdog" entities can also take a direction that veers from your intent. (Please see Chapter 7 for further details.)

Grantmaking and Your Intent

Of course, the optimal outcome is to develop a culture that instinctively honors donor intent, one that informs the work not only of your board but also that of your executive director and staff as they go about their day-to-day grantmaking. Nevertheless, it is important as well to take measures to ensure that individual grants fulfill donor intent. It is important, for example, to develop grantmaking guidelines that are in concert with your intent and that clearly communicate the founder's intentions to potential grantees. Such documents also provide meaningful guidance for program officers and others within your organization, illustrating for them how donor intent becomes operational in the grantmaking process.

The same attention to donor intent should take place in evaluating the performance of grants. At the Arthur N. Rupe Foundation, for example, grant evaluations written by the program officer include a section on how the grant advanced the foundation's mission. These evaluations are reviewed by the board to ensure that the foundation's grantmaking is in line with the founder's intentions.

Board members can also act as important communicators of your charitable intentions to the charitable organizations that your philanthropy supports. In fact at some small and family foundations, board members, rather than staff, cultivate the principal relationships between the foundation and the grantees. In some cases, board members are under considerable pressure from organizations to advance their application for approval with their board, even when it does not fit precisely within the parameters of the donor's intent. This is an unavoidable fact of the philanthropic world. Having clearly articulated donor-intent guidelines makes it much easier for director or trustees simply to say, "I'm sorry, it just doesn't fit what we fund."

Some foundations, in an effort to compensate their trustees and directors for their commitment and to remove the temptation of bringing proposals for pet projects or other proposals that do not align precisely with the foundation's mission to the board, give their directors discretionary grantmaking authority of a pre-determined amount. The John M. Olin Foundation, for example, had a policy of giving its directors what are sometimes called "board" or "chairman" grants, as do many other foundations. At the Olin Foundation, each board member was allowed to make grants of up to $25,000 (eventually the figure became $100,000).

Some foundations restrict board discretionary grants to the mission of their foundation. Some leave them open-ended. The argument for board discretionary grants is sometimes advanced based on the pragmatic argument that creating an outlet for modest, discretionary board grantmaking removes the temptation to bring such grants to the full consideration of the board, possibly distracting or even diluting the mission. It also recognizes that board members are often badgered with requests for money, even from organizations that have nothing to do with the charitable purpose of the foundation they serve. As a policy intended to help secure donor intent, board discretionary grants serve the purpose of making sure that such requests do not intrude on the principal business of the foundation.

Trust in the Future

There are many steps you can take to protect donor intent among your directors or trustees. All come with a caveat. Board policies that are intended to encourage loyalty should not be so excessive or overly detailed that they stifle engagement. Trustees must have a sense of what their title suggests—that you have some faith in their judgment. Board members who do not believe their contributions are valued may invest time on your board, but they will not invest much effort or imagination, nor will they in fact develop an allegiance to your mission. When possible, therefore, create and adopt policies that inspire and guide board members but that do not call into question their abilities or intentions.

CHAPTER 7
Creating External Safeguards to Protect Your Intent

The focus of this guidebook so far has been on establishing *internal* safeguards for preserving your charitable intentions: choosing the right legal entity; crafting a mission statement and making it operational; selecting strong board members and codifying the means for perpetuating them; and setting up board policies for preserving your intent.

If you set up your foundation early, grow it over time, establish a giving history and an operational framework, and provide for a sunset provision, then your internal safeguards greatly improve the chances that your philanthropic purposes will be secured as you intended. Nevertheless, are there also *external* safeguards for protecting donor intent that you should consider?

Perpetual entities exist for a very long time—"perpetuity is a lot longer than you think," as the old line goes—with limited safeguards for preserving the intent of a since-deceased donor. Indeed, grantmaking entities have even fewer external oversight controls than public charities. After all, public charities are accountable to the funders who support them. A grantmaking institution whose donor is no longer living lacks even this minimal external corrective mechanism. Who will hold your board members to account if they depart from the charitable mission of your foundation?

By law, a grantmaking entity is held accountable by the Attorney General in the state in which it is domiciled. A state Attorney General typically has the statutory duty to oversee all charitable organizations within his or her state. But the Attorney General may or may not intervene if your charitable entity departs from its mission. For one thing, states spend very little time and resources monitoring grantmakers. For another, they tend only to get involved when there are allegations of fraud or other criminal activity. In other words, while the Attorney General has statutory oversight, it is unlikely that he will intervene if the mission of a grantmaking entity begins to veer off course.

Furthermore, even when an Attorney General does act, there is no guarantee that his intervention will preserve the purpose of a foundation. The record is mixed. The Attorney General serves and acts on behalf of the public interest. It is not inconceivable, or even necessarily unlikely, that an Attorney General could interpret your donor intent restrictions to be contrary to the public interest.

For these reasons, some donors who establish perpetual giving entities have taken additional steps to protect their charitable intentions by creating external,

The Problem of Standing

One complicating factor in creating external donor intent safe-guards is the problem of standing. "Standing" is a legal term, signifying that a party has a definable legal interest in a matter. A court will not recognize a party's ability to bring legal action if that party lacks standing. In some states—Connecticut, for example—the courts have decided that even *donors* do not have standing to bring an action in court to enforce their intent.

As Paul Rhoads argues in *Starting a Private Foundation*, "it is not possible to state categorically that one may grant legal standing to external individuals or organizations." With private trusts, there are clear beneficiaries who automatically have standing to take action against the trust and trustees. Charitable trusts and corporate entities, however, seldom have named beneficiaries. As such, it is unclear whether a court will grant standing to a third party who is not a beneficiary, even if the trust instrument or corporate document gives someone the authority to go to court to enforce donor intent.

In one instance cited by Rhoads—the Barnes Foundation case—a Pennsylvania court granted standing to a third party in addition to the Attorney General. Standing was given because the third party met the state law's criteria governing standing: the individual had "relevant origin," a substantive and legitimate relationship to the foundation, a record of significant contributions to the foundation, and a "real interest" in the issue in being litigated. Standings are fact-specific cases, however, and the Barnes example does not at all suggest a clear path for obtaining third-party standing by donors. States may permit standing for persons with a "special interest" in the issue or to stand in place of the Attorney General as a relator, but courts interpret special interest narrowly and seldom have granted standing for relators.

third-party safeguards. A range of external safeguards may be contemplated. In some instances, donors have incorporated into their governing instrument provisions that give board members standing to bring suit for violations of donor intent. Others have given standing to disinterested third-party organizations that share the donor's principles. Still others have stipulated that their boards include third-party representatives from sympathetic organizations. And finally, at least one major foundation has incorporated regular donor intent audits.

These third-party "watchdogs" assume responsibility to enforce future compliance with your charitable intentions. They can even go so far as to sue your board members, if necessary. For donors planning a perpetual entity, independent safeguards offer another layer of oversight. It is important to keep in mind that few independent safeguards have been put to the legal test. Still, there may be good reasons for creating such safeguards, even if ultimately they do not survive a legal challenge.

While recognizing that simply granting authority to a third party to enforce donor intent may not in itself meet the necessary legal threshold for standing, some foundations have pursued this strategy in conjunction with other measures as a way of protecting donor intent.

Giving Standing to Outside Parties

Thomas A. Roe was a South Carolinian businessman who used his philanthropy to help establish a movement of state-focused, free-market think tanks across the country. Attentive to donor intent, Roe carefully implemented a range of internal mechanisms to protect his intentions when he established the Roe Foundation. He clearly spelled out his foundation's mission, his beliefs, and his general philosophical principles in his founding documents. He carefully chose board members who shared his beliefs and who subscribed in writing to the foundation's mission and to the principles of donor intent. He required the same of his grantees, asking them to pledge in writing to uphold the mission of the foundation and his donor intent.

Finally, Roe named as watchdogs two organizations that he knew well and that shared his philosophical outlook. He granted these two organizations—the Mont Pelerin Society and the Philadelphia Society—and any of their directors standing to challenge the foundation in court, were it to violate donor intent or its announced principles.

Roe also insisted that these two organizations, in addition to being granted standing to sue, remain substantial beneficiaries of the foundation, receiving annual grants. This second provision—giving two organizations meaningful contributions each year—makes them, in effect, quasi-beneficiaries with a special interest in the conduct of the foundation.

There is no guarantee, were litigation ever to be brought by one or both of the two watchdog organizations, that they would be granted standing in court. In a strictly legal sense, neither organization is truly a "beneficiary." Nevertheless, the example of the Roe Foundation is instructive for those seeking to establish third-party safeguards.

One important thing to remember is that Roe was active in both the Mont Pelerin Society and the Philadelphia Society during his lifetime. He had good reason to believe they share his philosophical outlook and, unlike a grantmaker, would be held accountable to their mission by their membership and other donors. If the foundation ever changed course, presumably the board members of either organization would step in to resolve the issue.

Whether or not a judge would give either organization standing is an open question. Regardless, there are good reasons for establishing third-party oversight. For one thing, their presence alone acts as a safeguard for donor intent, as they are a constant reminder to the board of what Roe meant to accomplish through his charitable giving. They constantly remind those associated with the Roe Foundation: These are the organizations that were meaningful to Roe. Finally, their inclusion in the foundation's bylaws is a not-so-subtle reminder to the foundation's board members that they can be held to account by outside parties.

Incorporating Sympathetic Organizations into Your Board

Another strategy for creating independent safeguards for a perpetual grantmaking entity is to make provision in the bylaws (or other establishing documents) for representation on the board by organizations that share the organization's mission. Under this scenario, board representatives from third-party organizations are supposed to ensure that the grantmaker's activities support the donor's intentions as stated in the mission statement. As board members, they have standing to bring suit against the board if it takes a direction contrary to its stated purpose. Some observers have even suggested that donors stipulate that a majority of board members be drawn from one or more charitable organizations that share the foundation's mission. At minimum, they would act as watchdogs for donor intent.

For example, upon her death, Clare Boothe Luce, the widow of *Time* and *Fortune* founder Henry R. Luce, established through a bequest the Clare Boothe Luce Program at the Luce Foundation. The program today is the single most significant source of private support for women in science, mathematics, and engineering. Knowing how foundations can veer in their missions once the founder is no longer involved, Luce stipulated that the governing body of the newly formed entity comprise individuals, at least in part, from organizations that she knew and trusted: people whom she knew would carry out her intentions as she wished. As such, she stipulated that three of the representatives on the board come from the Heritage Foundation, an organization in which she was actively involved and whose mission she eagerly supported.

An alternative to appointing a majority of board members from third-party organizations is to make a provision in your bylaws that requires a supermajority to amend the bylaws, particularly to make changes to the foundation's mission or purpose. This would give the minority of board members from third-party organizations, the watchdog directors, the ability to effectively veto any changes in the foundation's mission.

There are, however, serious potential drawbacks to consider in giving third-party organizations influence over your grantmaking entity. First, organizations sometimes drift from their mission in ways that cannot be anticipated. For this reason, it is important to consider carefully the organizations that you involve in your board, including their mission, their history, and their own provisions for ensuring that they pursue their stated purpose. Second, representatives from outside organizations, especially if only one such organization is represented on your board, may try to sway support to their organization. Finally, the representative organization may simply cease to exist. In this instance, a provision may require the foundation's board to choose another representative organization or simply let the position sit vacant, eliminating the influence that you tried to create in setting aside the seat.

Instituting Donor Intent Audits

The John Templeton Foundation provides an additional example of innovative ways to create independent donor intent safeguards.

When John M. Templeton Sr. established the foundation, he took great care in creating internal safeguards to ensure that his intentions for the foundation would be carried out over time. Aside from crafting a well-wrought mission, he stipulated in the foundation's charter and bylaws what the foundation would and would not fund. He required the foundation's board of trustees to read the charter annually, knowing that once he was no longer involved in the foundation that the trustees would be the governing authority. Moreover, the trustees oversee each grant and program specifically to ensure that they comport with donor intent.

Sir John also reportedly stipulated that every five years the trustees must oversee an external audit process to evaluate whether or not the foundation's grantmaking is in keeping with the provisions of the bylaws and charter. If the audit finds that less than 91 percent of all grants align with donor intent, the directors put the officers of the foundation on probation for one year. If the foundation again fails to meet the 91 percent threshold in a subsequent audit, the trustees are empowered to remove the officers.

The audit is exceptional in that it has actual consequences for those who run the foundation. The audit not only forces the foundation to independently assess its giving in terms of donor intent at regular intervals, it forces staff, officers, and trustees to perpetually ask how a given grant is fulfilling the mission of the foundation. It provides a prudential check on the organization by making donor intent central to its day-to-day grantmaking activities. In other words, it makes donor intent operational, not simply aspirational.

The foundation has yet to undergo a donor-intent audit, as the provision in the charter that stipulates the audit was not triggered until after Sir John's death (in 2008). Like any audit, the outcome of a donor-intent audit is contingent, at least in part, upon the mandate given to, and the competency of, the auditors. Furthermore, assessing whether or not a grant fulfills donor intent is at least in part a subjective enterprise. Perhaps the most ambitious grants, the ones that would best suit the donor's intentions, will prove the most difficult to assess. If an individual grant fulfills 90 percent of the donor's intention, rather than 91 percent, will it be considered a failed grant? How difficult will it be to assign these percentages?

Meaningful Oversight, Not Ongoing Conflict
Creating external safeguards can be an effective way of holding directors and trustees accountable to donor intent in perpetual giving entities. It is important to keep in mind, however, that it is also possible to go too far in creating independent safeguards, undermining your board members or creating a perception that they are either not trusted or not ultimately responsible for the well-being of the foundation. It is probably best to seek a prudent balance between establishing independent safeguards and instilling your trustees with a sense of responsibility. As Paul Rhoads writes, "one wants to encourage future trustees, and establish an esprit de corps that develops loyalty to the foundation's mission."

It is also important to consider establishing external safeguards in conjunction with your tolerance for flexibility. The independent safeguards that you choose should reflect your views on how much or how little flexibility your trustees will have to adapt or modify the mission of the foundation to accommodate future change. Where there is little tolerance for trustee flexibility in this regard, the independent safeguards should be strong. If your trustees are given great flexibility in adapting the foundation to changing circumstances, the safeguards that you establish should reflect this fact.

Finally, there is a subjective aspect to donor intent which ought to be considered. While a clearly articulated mission statement can and ought to delineate clearly a donor's purposes and goals, disagreement can and will arise among well-intentioned parties as to whether or not a specific grant or program fulfills a donor's intent, even when that intent is made plain. Donors should take care in creating external safeguards to ensure that they are establishing meaningful oversight rather than ongoing conflict between trustees and third-party interests.

CONCLUSION

When a donor's wishes are compromised, it's frequently the case that the donor did not make his charitable intent clear enough. No document, regardless of how well it is put together, will absolutely guarantee that donor intent will be maintained over time. Indeed, a trust instrument or corporate document that tries too hard to anticipate every future contingency can unwittingly undermine the ability of future directors and trustees to carry out the founder's charitable intent by being too specific and inflexible. At the same time, donors often err by making their directives too open-ended, giving future trustees and directors little guidance in creating an operational strategy.

Beyond that, if you want to preserve your intentions, you will need to be proactive in planning your giving entity. Start early, even if that means starting small. Donors who play an active role in making their philanthropic mission operational in their lifetimes have a better track record in preserving their intentions over time.

As this guidebook explains, you can minimize the deleterious effects that time can have on your intentions by choosing the right giving vehicle for your philanthropy; by limiting the life of your giving entity; by memorializing your intentions through a carefully thought-through mission statement; by choosing and cultivating the right people to perpetuate your philanthropy; by adopting board policies crafted to instill donor intent; and by creating external safeguards to preserve your intentions.

By taking these steps, you can have a reasonable expectation that your philanthropy will serve the purposes that originally inspired you to give.

For more resources and information, please visit

ProtectingDonorIntent.com

ABOUT THE PHILANTHROPY ROUNDTABLE

The Philanthropy Roundtable is a national association of individual donors, corporate giving officers, and foundation staff and trustees. The Roundtable attracts philanthropists who benefit from being part of an organization dedicated to helping them achieve their charitable objectives. In addition to offering expert advice and counsel, the Roundtable puts donors in touch with peers who share similar concerns and interests. Members of the Roundtable gain access to a donor community interested in philanthropic freedom, innovation, and excellence.

Mission

The mission of The Philanthropy Roundtable is to foster excellence in philanthropy, protect philanthropic freedom, help donors achieve their philanthropic intent, and assist donors in advancing liberty, opportunity, and personal responsibility in America and abroad.

Principles

- Voluntary private action offers solutions for many of society's most pressing challenges.
- A vibrant private sector is critical for generating the wealth that makes philanthropy possible.
- Excellence in philanthropy is measured by results, not good intentions.
- A respect for donor intent is essential for philanthropic integrity.
- Philanthropic freedom is essential to a free society.

Services

Annual Meeting

The Roundtable has long been known for the quality of its conferences, foremost among them the Annual Meeting. The Annual Meeting is the Roundtable's flagship event, where leading donors, executives, and trustees from across the country meet to share ideas, strategies, and best practices, and hear from America's foremost experts in private innovation and forward-thinking solutions.

Regional Meetings

The Roundtable's Breakthrough Groups host regular regional meetings and dinners. These conferences are held in different cities throughout the year, bringing together donors to discuss issues of common concern. Many donors find that these smaller, more focused meetings enable them to better network with peers who share similar concerns and interests.

Philanthropy magazine

The Roundtable's publications are essential reading for donors committed to freedom, opportunity, and personal responsibility. Each issue of the Roundtable's quarterly magazine, *Philanthropy*, offers donors insights into topics of significance in the charitable sector, focuses on broad strategic questions in line with our principles, and provides real guidance and clear examples of effective philanthropy.

Guidebooks

The Roundtable's guidebooks are in-depth examinations of the principled and practical aspects of charitable giving. Our guidebooks connect donors with the best information available for achieving philanthropic excellence. The Roundtable publishes new guidebooks every year and provides free copies to qualified donors.

Alliance for Charitable Reform

Through its Alliance for Charitable Reform (ACR), the Roundtable works with legislators, policymakers, and interest groups in support of philanthropic freedom. ACR is dedicated to educating policymakers on contributions of American private philanthropy, its longstanding tradition and the role it plays in their communities. It also works to help members communicate their message effectively, and to encourage thought, discussion, and debate on issues related to charity and public policy.

Consulting and Referral Services

Members of the Roundtable benefit from the insights and experience of their peers. Many of our members have agreed to serve as informal advisors to their Roundtable colleagues. To fulfill donor interests outside of the scope of our mission and activities, the Roundtable collaborates with other philanthropic-service organizations or refers donors directly to other experts.

ABOUT THE AUTHOR

Jeffrey J. Cain is president and executive director of the Santa Barbara, California–based Arthur N. Rupe Foundation. He is also secretary of the Lillian S. Wells Foundation, executive publisher of *Philanthropy Daily*, and founding partner at American Philanthropic. Prior to joining the Rupe Foundation, Mr. Cain served as executive vice president at the Intercollegiate Studies Institute, a national educational nonprofit committed to advancing a traditional liberal arts curriculum and the study of Western civilization. Mr. Cain previously taught in the English department at Washington State University (where he received his M.A. and Ph.D. in English literature), founded a research nonprofit (the Columbia Public Interest Policy Institute), worked on various political campaigns in his native state of Washington, and served in the United States Marine Corps.